A **Rose**: The Layers In A Transformation Process

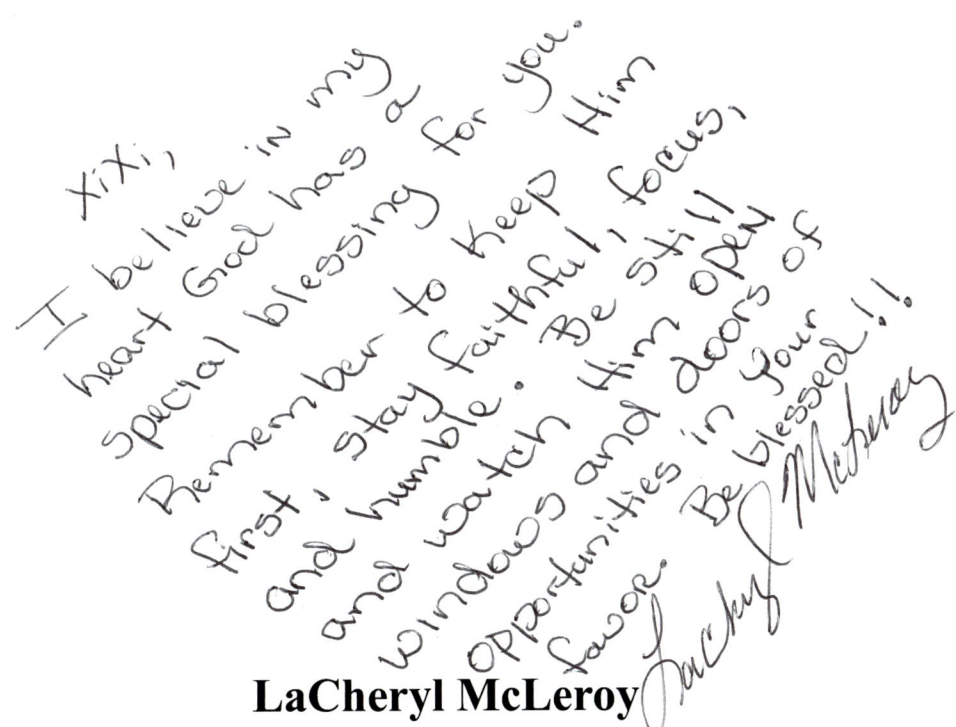

LaCheryl McLeroy

Copyright © 2020 LaCheryl McLeroy

ISBN: 978-0-578-67836-8

All rights reserved. All rights reserved. No part of this publication may be reproduced or transmitted in any form or by any means, including photocopying, recording, or other electronic or mechanical methods, without written permission of the author, except in case of brief quotations embodied in critical reviews and certain other noncommercial uses permitted by copyright laws-. For permission requests, contact LaCheryl McLeroy @ 316-200-8567 for further information.

This is a work of nonfiction. Any resemblance to actual events or persons, living or dead, is entirely coincidental.

Spiritual Mentor/Editor: A. Brown

Proofreader: Herbert Powell

Cover Illustration and Graphic Designer: Marvin D. Ginyard (prolyfyk@gmail.com)

Marketing Director: LaSydra Powell

Scripture taken from the New King James Version®. Copyright © 1982 by Thomas Nelson. Used by permission. All rights reserved.

Scripture taken from The Holy Bible, NEW INTERNATIONAL VERSION®, NIV® Copyright© 1973,1978, 1984, 2011 by Biblica, Inc. ® Used by permission. All rights reserved worldwide.

Scriptures quotations are taken from the Holy Bible, New Living Translation, copyright© 1996, 2004, 2015 by Tyndale House Foundation. Used by permission of Tyndale House Publishers, Inc., Carol Stream, Illinois 60188. All rights reserved.

All Scripture quotations are taken from The Message copyright© 1993, 2002, 2018 by Eugene H. Peterson. Used by permission of NavPress. All rights reserved. Represented by Tyndale House Publishers, Inc.

DEDICATION

In loving memory of Mattie Mae McElroy (Grandmother) and Mattie Ruth McLeroy (Mother). Through their life experiences, they have taught me how to stand firm in every adversity. They also taught me never to give up when times get tough, always to love family and friends unconditionally while maintaining a spiritual connection with our Heavenly Father above. Through the structured environment, which they created, instilled valuable principles within me, which I still use today. Even though we had many disagreements concerning the matters of the heart, I never stopped loving them both. Through their unconditional loving sacrifices, our family legacy will live on forever. For that, I say, "Thank You," to both, for being two loving and robust role models.

"She speaks with wisdom, and faithful instruction is on her tongue."
Proverbs 31:26 (NIV)

CONTENTS

Acknowledgements

Introduction

Chapter One: Site - The Breaking Ground	1
Chapter Two: Soil - Removal of Weeds (Sins)	14
Chapter Three: Mulch - Seeds of Life	32
Chapter Four: Water - Seasons	43
Chapter Five: Inspections - Admiring the Beauty	58
Chapter Six: Prune - Priceless	71
Chapter Seven: Full Bloom	91
Chapter Eight: New Beginning	98
Final Words	104
Appendix	105

ACKNOWLEDGMENTS

I want to thank my Savior, Jesus Christ, who never stops loving and drawing me close to his heart even when I occasionally try to walk away from His path. I want to thank my Heavenly Father for allowing my path to cross with many Bishops, Apostles, Pastors, and Teachers of Christ. Through their powerful spoken words, they have watered life into a dormant seed and given birth to this book. I want to thank all my Spiritual Leaders, Mentors, and Sisters who are a part of the Purpose and Destiny KC organization, who prayed and ministered words of encouragement into my spirit. I want to thank my children, family, and close friends for always loving and encouraging me to achieve my dreams. I want to thank my Spiritual Editor, Proofreader, Graphic Designer, Marketing Director, and Ghostwriter for helping me birth this book and becoming an Author. Lastly, I want to thank my readers for purchasing this book and allowing God's word to minister life into your spirit.

"May the Lord richly bless both you and your children. May you be blessed by the Lord who made heaven and earth. The heavens belong to the Lord, but he has given the earth to all humanity."
Psalm 115:14-16 (NLT)

*Healing
that revitalizes the soul.
Calms the spirit during a storm.
Gives the abilities to call on the
Father for help when obstacles are
faced so, you can prosper in all
areas of your lives through hard
work, dedication, and
perseverance.*

Introduction

Every year across America on Valentine's Day, millions of dollars of stemmed roses are purchased. Throughout the year, billions of dollars of roses are sold in various colors with specific sentimental expression. At the time of purchase, deep thoughts flood the mind concerning what color rose to give; a feeling of emotional relief fills the heart after seeing the facial expression or hearing the gratification expressed by the person receiving a rose. God is the Rose of Sharon. His unconditional love for us shows in the color red. He shines yellow rays of sunshine that produce a feeling of joy. When his heartaches, tears flood the sky with blue to shower us with rain. His grace and mercy fill the darkening night with the stars and moon that shine the color white. God loves all colors. He showed Noah a rainbow in the sky as a promise that He would never again flood the Earth (Genesis 9). Based on the color chart below, what color(s) does God see in you? Why?

Colors	Sentimental Expression
Blue	Sympathy
Orange	Encourager, Warmhearted
Peach	Sincerity
Pink	Admiration
Red	Love
White	Purity/Virtues
Yellow	Joy/ Enthusiasm

    The day God created Heaven's atmosphere and Earth's foundation; white and red rose seeds of purity and love were embedded to strengthen the core. 2 Timothy 3:16-17 (NLT) says, "All Scripture is inspired by God and is useful to teach us what is true and to make us realize what is wrong in our lives. It corrects us when we are wrong and teaches us to do what is right. God uses it to prepare and equip his people to do every good work." The day Adam was created, God scooped up a handful of Earth remnants from the foundation to blow life into the soul of Adam before transferring the same foundation through a rib to create Eve. Through Adam and Eve's bloodline, all ancestors created after them would have the qualities of white and red rose seeds of purity and love.

    After placing Satan on Earth, black rose seeds of weeds (sins) began corrupting the foundation. God knew humanity would not last long, so He implanted a white and red rose seed of purity and love into a virgin named Mary. With this seed, she would give birth to the Savior of the world, Jesus Christ. John 3:16-17 (NIV) says," For God so loved the world that he gave his one and only Son, that whoever believes in him shall not perish but have eternal life. For God did not send his Son into the world to condemn the world, but to save the world through him." Jesus demonstrated, through His preaching, unselfish acts of purity and love before humanity crucified Him on the cross. A cross that was saturated with blood from His pierced and beaten naked body while dripping into the foundation of the world white and red rose seeds of purity and love. The Holy Spirit (Comforter) was sent to finish uprooting weeds (sins) through A Rose: The Layers In A Transformation Process. John 14:15-17 (NIV) says, "If you love me, keep my commands. And I will ask the Father and He will give you another advocate to help you and be with you forever-the Spirit of truth. The world cannot accept Him because it neither sees Him nor knows Him. But you know Him, for He lives with you and will be in you."

The Father's **D**N**A** (**D**angerous a**N**d **A**nointed)[1] spirit has always dwelled inside of us. Still, through Satan's tricky acts of deception, our flesh can now overpower our spirit if not anchored solidly in the word of God. The only way to restore the mind, body, and soul is to allow the Holy Spirit (Comforter) to assist the Father during the transformation process. Once restored, the vessel must continue to strengthen its foundation daily by praying and studying God's word. Eventually, in God's timing, a restored Chosen vessel[2] will be transformed into a Man of Valor or a Beautiful Butterfly ready to be used in God's mighty Army.

Seed for Thought: Are you ready to be transformed? If the answer is Yes, then take a moment to grant complete access to every area of your life to the Father. He can remove all the black rose seeds of weeds (sins) before revitalizing the white and red rose seeds of purity and love during A Rose: The Layers In A Transformation Process.

Chapter One

Site- The Breaking Ground

"I planted, Apollos watered, but God gave the increase. So then neither he who plants is anything, nor he who waters, but God who gives the increase. Now he who plants and he who waters are one, and each one will receive his own reward according to his own labor. For we are God's fellow workers; you are God's field, you are God's building. According to the grace of God, which was given to me, as a wise master builder, I have laid the foundation, and another builds on it. But let each one take heed how he builds on it. For no other foundation can anyone lay than that which is laid, which is Jesus Christ. "

1 Corinthians 3:6-11 (NKJV)

The Breaking Ground[3] is God, the Rose of Sharon (Song of Songs 2:1). A Rose that is delicate to touch, beautiful to admire, and powerful beyond measure with a lasting fragrance, linger on forever. Through a spoken word, Heaven's atmosphere and Earth's foundation were created (2 Timothy 2:19-21). With a gentle touch, the atmosphere beyond the universe created a covering for the sky, stars, moon, and Earth's foundation. After creating the foundation. White and red rose seeds of purity and love were embedded deep into Earth's core to provide nutrients to grow trees, grass, plants, flowers, and food to eat. Every type of species created either lived on the foundation, flew in the sky, or swam in the sea (Psalm 33:6,9). When God finished with everything, He said it was very good. Which means the first part of my job is done; I am going to go rest (Genesis 1; Proverbs 3:19-20).

Seed for Thought: Think about everything God created and supplied for man throughout the bible. Do you believe God can supply all your needs according to Philippians 4:19? If your answer is yes, on the lines below, tell God how thankful you are for providing all the necessity to live each day (1 Thessalonians 5:16-18).

_____

_____

_____

_____

_____

_____

_____

_____

_____

_____

After resting, God decided to blow life into the foundation to create Adam. His primary job was to preserve and protect the Garden of Eden while providing names to every type of species created. God knew Adam could not live alone, so He placed him into a deep sleep before detaching a rib from the inside of his body to form Eve. Again, God made sure all provisions were met for them to live a blessed and abundant life forever. The only rule given was to not eat any fruit from the tree of knowledge of good and evil (Genesis 2).

Seed for Thought: God uses His love to guard us against Satan's deceptive tactic instead of using a stern hand to punish us for being disobedient. Romans 8:12-13 (NLT) says, "Therefore, dear brothers and sisters, you have no obligation to do what your sinful nature urges you to do. For if you live by its dictates, you will die. But if through the power of the Spirit you put to death the deeds of your sinful nature, you will live." This is the only way to guarantee life's road will remain clear, straight, and narrow without distraction like the picture below.

Satan, an anointed guardian cherub and his followers, tried to use deceptive tactics to take over Heaven. Still, God blocked their plans and immediately administered judgment. He and his followers went from being adored by others to a spectacle, beauty consumed in the fire to produce ashes after being removed from Heaven and banished forever (Ezekiel

28:11-19). Out of anger towards God, Satan had his followers embed into Earth's core more black rose seeds of weeds (sins). Satan even convinced Eve to eat a piece of fruit from the tree of knowledge of good and evil. Immediately, after biting into the corrupted fruit, black rose seeds of weeds (sins) quickly spread into her mind. Scales started forming over her eyes to see a visible image of a naked body that needed clothes instead of a spiritual model that was not ashamed of being unclothed. Her flesh started craving unhealthy sinful desires, such as debauchery (unnecessary indulgence in sexual urges). While experiencing the emotion of hatred, fits of rage, jealousy, envy, and many other sinful pleasures that were not supposed to be revealed (Galatians 5:19-21).

Seed for Thought: Sin is a lot like misery that loves the company; the more you entertain the thoughts or actions; eventually, sin will affect your life and others around you. What do you think happened to Adam after Eve convinced him to eat from the tree of knowledge of good and evil? Stop right now and examine your heart. Do you have any corrupted areas that need releasing over to God?

_____

_____

_____

_____

Adam and Eve were God's first living instruments created to bear healthy fruit and act in accordance with the Holy standards established for humanity (John 15:16). When the rules became tainted with black rose seeds of weeds (sins), God had no choice but to show his mighty stern hand to prove He meant business for disobeying His word. First, He revoked Adam and Eve's privileges to use the Garden of Eden forever. Second, because of Adam, men would forever work hard labor to provide a decent lifestyle for their families. Third, because of Eve, women will forever experience excruciating labor pains during childbirth. Fourth, the chief suspect Satan would no longer walk but crawl on his belly indefinitely (Genesis 3).

One brisk spring Sunday morning around 8:00 a.m., I decided to take a walk around the lake near my apartment. When I reached a small wood bridge at the entrance of the walking trail, the Holy Spirit (Comforter) prompted me to stop, close my eyes, and meditate on God's grace and mercy. While standing with my eyes closed, I could hear the birds chirping and the ducks quacking while envisioning God's majestic beauty that surrounded me. At that moment, a slight breeze gently rubbed my body, causing the hairs on my arms to rise. Feeling the master's touch gave me a sense of joy and peace at the same time, knowing He chose to love on me this morning. A love so strong that He desires that no man should perish but spend eternity with Him forever. Which requires humanity to release control and grant complete access so.....

The Breaking Ground

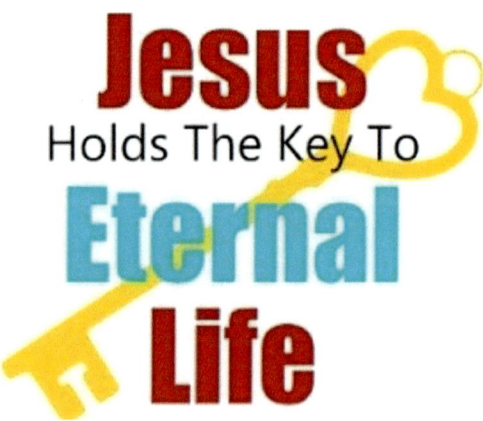

    The foundation which God created was no longer pure and loving but tarnished with the choice to either serve God or the flesh. Having so many options embedded in the minds of individuals makes it difficult to justify and release complete control to an omnipresent God. Romans 1:20-21 (NIV) says, "For since the creation of the world, God's invisible qualities-his eternal power and divine nature-have been clearly seen, being understood from what has been made, so that people are without excuse. For although they knew God, they neither glorified Him as God nor gave thanks to Him, but their thinking became futile and their foolish hearts were darkened." Once the mind becomes corrupted with sin, unhealthy emotion fills the heart to weaken the spirit to resent God for every painful mistake and failure made that produced a crappy life.

Seed for Thought: Fulfilling sinful pleasures of the flesh will only disrupt the master's original plan for our life. Stop and exam your heart to see if you are interrupting the master's plan. Jeremiah 29:11 (NIV) says, "For I know the plans I have for you," declares the Lord, "plans to prosper you and not to harm you, plans to give you hope and a future" that will sow an abundance of blessing for being obedient instead of reaping curses for being disobedient.

Obedience sows Blessing

"Let all that I am praise the Lord; may I never forget the good things he does for me. He forgives all my sins and heals all my diseases. He redeems me from death and crowns me with love and tender mercies He fills my life with good things. My youth is renewed like the eagle's! " Psalm 103:2-5 (NLT)

Obedience requires repenting and turning away from sin, so God can place the vessel on the Potter's wheel to be transformed. A process that may take the rest of your life to complete. Jeremiah 31:19 (NLT) says, "I turned away from God, but then I was sorry. I kicked myself for my stupidity! I was thoroughly ashamed of all I did in my younger days." God's precious anointed mighty words, spoken and written, can heal and restore the mind, sustain the body from sin, and place a covering over the soul, so the spirit will trust, obey, and remain faithful to inherit eternal life with the Father forever (Psalm 119). God does His best work when a willing vessel, out of obedience, surrenders their whole body as a living sacrifice. Romans 12:1-2 (NIV) says, "Therefore, I urge you, brothers and sisters, in view of God's mercy, to offer your bodies as a living sacrifice, holy and pleasing to God—this is your true and proper worship. Do not conform to the pattern of this world but be transformed by the renewing of your mind. Then you will be able to test and approve what God's will is—his good, pleasing and perfect will."

Seed for Thought: Obedience is not something you can earn through a reward system or purchase from a local store but an action that requires completely surrendering and trusting your will to a higher authority. Who do you believe? Is it the Father or the Flesh? Why? (Proverbs 3:5-6)

_____

_____

_____

_____

Submitting to God's plan in obedience caused Moses, Noah, Abraham, Joseph, and the twelve disciples along with Ruth, Esther, Deborah, and others to sacrifice their time, talent, and treasure to carry out the master's ultimate plan. A plan that would bless them abundantly as well as receive the crown of righteousness in eternity for fighting the good fight, finishing the course, and keeping the faith (2 Timothy 4:7-8). Also, through their obedience, God opened the windows of Heaven to pour out an abundance of blessings on everything they touched, created, and produced (Deuteronomy 28:1-14; Matthew 6:19-21). Even their enemies became their footstool. Proverbs 16:7 (NKJV), "When a man's ways please the Lord, He makes even his enemies to be at peace with him."

Seed for Thought: Obedience out of love and admiration to God will cause you to alter your plans to fulfill His ultimate plan. Such as quitting a meaningless job to start a God-ordained business, writing a book, relocating to an unfamiliar place, or letting go of people and material possessions put in place of God. What has the Father asked you to do for Him that you keep avoiding? (Luke 11:28) On the space below, jot down what the Holy Spirit (Comforter) is telling you to do.

_____

_____

_____

_____

The Bible tells a story about a young man named Joseph. When he was a young boy, there was a special calling on his life. Jacob, his father knew it. His brothers sold him into slavery out of jealousy. With Joseph not around, the brothers figured their father would focus on them, which never happened. God favored Joseph. Everything he touched or produced was blessed. Joseph, as a slave, went from running the jailhouse to overseeing the big house that belonged to Pharaoh after interpreting a dream. For seven years, Egypt was blessed abundantly under Joseph's command. When a famine fell on the land, there was enough food stored up to sell and make more money for Pharaoh. Joseph's brothers had to travel to Egypt to buy food after a famine swept over the land. Never once, while purchasing food, did the brothers realize Joseph was alive and in charge of the storehouse. Joseph recognized his brothers and decided to test them several times before revealing his identity to the family and Jacob before he died (Genesis 37- 45).

Seed for Thought: Joseph demonstrated love through the act of obedience. According to Romans 12:9-21 (NIV) "Love must be sincere. Hate what is evil; cling to what is good. Be devoted to one another in love. Honor one another above yourselves. Never be lacking in zeal, but keep your spiritual fervor, serving the Lord. Be joyful in hope, patient in affliction, faithful in prayer. Share with the Lord's people who are in need. Practice hospitality. Bless those who persecute you; bless and do not curse. Rejoice with those who rejoice; mourn with those who mourn. Live in harmony with one another. Do not be proud but be willing to associate with people of low position. Do not be conceited. Do not repay anyone evil for evil. Be careful to do what is right in the eyes of everyone. If it is possible, as far as it depends on you, live at peace with everyone. " Do not take revenge, my dear friends, but leave room for God's wrath, for it is written: "It is mine to avenge; I will repay," says the Lord. On the contrary: "If your enemy is hungry, feed him; if he is thirsty, give him something to drink. In doing this, you will heap burning coals on his head. Do not be overcome by evil but overcome evil with good." Based on this scripture, how do you demonstrate love, so your life will reap blessings instead of curses?

_____

_____

_____

_____

Disobedience reaps Curses

"For the children of Israel walked forty years in the wilderness, till all the people who were men of war, who came out of Egypt, were consumed, because they did not obey the voice of the Lord—to whom the Lord swore that He would not show them the land which the Lord had sworn to their fathers that He would give us, "a land flowing with milk and honey."

Joshua 5:6 (NKJV)

Anyone who defies rules that are already set in place by an authority figure is a disobedient individual. The day God embedded white and red rose seeds of purity and love into the foundation, laws, and commandments were established. Adam and Eve broke those established rules the day their spirits became lukewarm. Having a lukewarm personality alters an individual behavior, which causes an individual to behave wrongfully or commit a sinful act. Eventually, if God is not allowed to intervene, the individual will harden their heart towards God and not hear His voice. Titus 1:16 (NLT) says, "Such people claim they know God, but they deny him by the way they live. They are detestable and disobedient, worthless for doing anything good." Choosing to be disobedient against God will cause your home, business, children, and their offspring to reap curses (Deuteronomy 28:15-68).

God does not like administering curses to anyone without giving numerous chances or warning signs to get it right.

Seed for Thought: Being obedient sows blessing and inherits eternal life. God will tell you on judgment day, "Well done, thy good and faithful servant"(Matthew 25:23). Being disobedient reaps damnation and God telling you, "I never knew you. Away from me, you evildoers!" (Matthew 7:23). If judgment day was to happen today, where would you go, Heaven or Hell? Why?

_____

_____

_____

_____

_____

_____

_____

The Bible tells us in Genesis 19, Abraham pleaded with God numerous times to have mercy on anyone worth saving in Sodom and Gomorrah. God agreed but made sure Abraham knew committing sinful acts was the reason He was administering judgment on the city. God selected Two Angels (foreigners) to carry out His master's plan. As the Angels (foreigners) approached the town, Lot went out to greet them with open arms. Lot, from a distance, noticed two lustful men staring at the Angels (foreigners). Immediately, Lot hurried the two Angels (foreigners) into the house before the sensual men got to the front door. Lot went outside and gave the lustful men an alternative to sleep with his two daughters instead of the two Angels (foreigners), but the men disagreed. The Angels (foreigners) became easily irritated and disgusted with the promiscuous acts performed in Sodom and Gomorrah. The lustful men's eyesight was blinded before they could bang on the front door. God remembered the promise made to Abraham to show mercy on anyone worth saving. The two Angels (foreigners) told Lot to take anyone worthy with him from Sodom and Gomorrah, not to look back or else they would die. As Lot and his family were fleeing Sodom and Gomorrah. His wife decided to look back. God turned her into a pillar of salt for being disobedient. God made numerous attempts to warn the people in Sodom and Gomorrah before destroying the city.

Seed for Thought: Is God telling you to let go of the past so that you can move forward? That means He has a bigger and better plan for your life that requires you completely trusting and obeying His word. I challenge everyone to read the entire chapter of Deuteronomy 28. After reading the chapter, take a few minutes to jot down any weeds (sins) God is revealing to you that is blocking living a blessed life (James 1:22-25).

Chapter Two

Soil-Removal of Weeds (Sins)

"For I will forgive their iniquity, and their sins will I remember no more."
Jeremiah 31:34 NLT

Removal of weeds (sins) requires granting access to the Father, so He can help you release every stronghold that holds you hostage. All strongholds that attach to the mind convince the spirit not to fear or respect God. Roman 3:18 (NKJV) says, "There is no fear of God before their eyes." Lacking fear causes an individual to commit temporary pleasures of the flesh (Romans 6:23), which creates a wicked heart (Matthew 9:4). Having no respect for God makes it easy to conform to false doctrines or people (1 Corinthians 15:33). Strongholds are wolves disguised in sheep's clothing (Matthew 7:15). Their only mission in life is to destroy or alter God's original plans. 2 Corinthians 10:3-6 (NKJV) says, "For though we walk in the flesh, we do not war according to the flesh. For the weapons of our warfare are not carnal but mighty in God for pulling down strongholds, casting down arguments and every high thing that exalts itself against the knowledge of God, bringing every thought into captivity to the obedience of Christ, and being ready to punish all disobedience when your obedience is fulfilled."

Seeds for Thought: Love can cast out any weeds (sins) that cause imperfection before turning into perfection. What imperfection are you withholding from the Father? (1 John 4:18-19)

_____

_____

_____

_____

What is a stronghold? A stronghold is a lie Satan uses to hold people in bondage. It can also be a place or material possession used by a person to convince the victim they cannot do any better than their current situation. A stronghold is dangerous and detrimental to anyone's life if left untreated. The only treatment is to allow God to place the individual on the Potter's wheel to teach, remove, and restore during the transformation process. James 3:13-18 (NIV) says, "Who is wise and understanding among you? Let them show it by their good life, by deeds done in the humility that comes from wisdom. But if you harbor bitter envy and selfish ambition in your hearts, do not boast about it or deny the truth. Such "wisdom" does not come down from heaven but is earthly, unspiritual, demonic. For where you have envy and selfish ambition, there you find disorder and every evil practice. But the wisdom that comes from heaven is first of all pure; then peace-loving, considerate, submissive, full of mercy and good fruit, impartial and sincere. Peacemakers who sow in peace reap a harvest of righteousness." To receive the fullness of God, we must first learn about the many strongholds that fall under the three main categories: Fear, Lack of Trust, and Unforgiveness.

- **Fear** has many names, such as worry, fright, scared, anxiety, concern, panic, cowardice, phobia, and distress. Fear makes it hard to grasp an understanding of any situation. Fear makes a person feel worthless and not worthy to receive everything God has in store for them. Fear bombards the mind and cripples the heart into remembering all failure, hurt, and disappointment, along with every negative word spoken over their life. If you do not face your fears head-on, eventually it will produce panic attacks, mental health issues, sickness, and even death. 2 Timothy 1:7 (KJV) says, "For God hath not given us the spirit of fear; but of power, and of love, and of a sound mind." God also tells us in Isaiah 41:10 (NIV), "So do not fear, for I am with you; do not be dismayed, for I am your God. I will strengthen you and help you; I will uphold you with my righteous right hand."

Seed for Thought: The best way to conquer all fear is to have great faith to believe you are an overcomer through the blood of Jesus. Who rules your life, fear or faith? Why is it hard to release? (Psalm 56:3-4)

- **Lack** of Trust is often known as unbelief, uncertainty, and rejection. Trust issues can be developed during a dysfunctional relationship, going through a bad divorce or betrayed by someone for selfish reasons. Lack of trust keeps the mind in bondage through fear of being hurt again. Lack of trust causes an individual to focus on wrong instead of right when the heart is hurting from past mistakes. Especially when mistrust is linked to emotional instability. Which makes it hard to commit to a healthy, loving relationship with God or people. Joshua 1:9 (NIV) says, "Be strong and courageous! Do not be afraid or discouraged. For the Lord your God is with you wherever you go." God also tells us in Psalm 34:8 (NIV), "Taste and see that the Lord is good; blessed is the one who takes refuge in him."

Seed for Thought: Building trust requires action instead of just saying words individuals want to hear. If your closest friends or family were to describe you, would trustworthy be one of the many words used? Why? (Proverbs 29:25)

- **Unforgiveness** manifests spirits of bitterness, frustration, and hatred. Unforgiveness clouds the vision and drains the soul until the mind starts to remember every slip-up or unresolved past matters that produces a feeling of guilt and shame. If God is not allowed to uproot any harmful toxins associated with unforgiveness, the physical body could experience serious health issues. Matthew 6:14-15 (NLT) "If you forgive those who sin against you, your heavenly Father will forgive you. But if you refuse to forgive others, your Father will not forgive your sins."

Seed for Thought: Anytime the enemy throws unforgiveness in your pathway, step back and say this quote below before reacting. "I forgive you, not because I'm ok with what you did or I'm cosigning to your version of events, but because I have to step away and get back to me. I must let go. It's not worth destroying me to prove a point or hold my anger" (Baggage Reclaim).[4] First, pray and ask the Holy Spirit (Comforter) to reveal any unforgiveness. Use the space below to reflect on what the Holy Spirit (Comforter) is telling you concerning unforgiveness.

_____
_____
_____
_____

    Fear, lack of trust, and unforgiveness will always lead an individual down a destructive path. A pathway that leaves behind trails of open wounds, emotional scars, and broken hearts. The longer sin remains untouched; the soul starts to look like the untreated, filthy, and nasty swimming pool pictured on the next page if God is not in the midst. Psalm 51:1-2

(NLT), "Have mercy on me, O God, because of your unfailing love. Because of your great compassion, blot out the stain of my sins. Wash me clean from my guilt. Purify me from my sin."

The Bible tells us in Genesis 25:19-34, about a young man named Isaac. Isaac interceded on Rebekah's behalf for children. The Lord honored Isaac's prayers, Rebekah conceived twins. While pregnant, she asked the Lord a question. Why do her unborn children struggle with one another? The LORD responded; two nations live inside you. The older will serve the younger. Rebekah gave birth to two sons; the first son named Esau because he had reddish hair with hairy skin, and the second son named Jacob. As the doctor was taking Esau out of the womb, Jacob held tightly onto the heel of his foot. Esau, when he was older, became a skilled hunter who loved the outdoors. Jacob was quiet and loved being indoors with his mother learning to cook. Isaac favored Esau, and Rebekah favored Jacob. Jacob one day was cooking a pot of bean soup when Esau came in from hunting and was very hungry. Jacob manipulated Esau to give up his birthright in exchange for a bowl of soup and a piece of bread. Esau agreed.

Seed for Thought: Everyone, from time to time, has used manipulation as a tactic to cheat or trick people into giving up or doing something they regret. Any decision made, whether good or bad, will either reap consequences of destruction or sow blessings into their life. Ask yourself the five simple questions below to determine if God is leading you or your flesh is in control.

- **Did** the plans I created involve God or just me?

_____
_____
_____
_____

- **Who** did I use or hurt to achieve my success?

_____
_____
_____
_____

- **Why** did I take the route I took? Could it be that I allowed people to influence my every thought or decision I made?

_____
_____
_____
_____

- **When** did the driving force to achieving power become so strong in my life?

_____
_____
_____
_____

- **What** effect did my plans have on me as well as the people I hold dear to my heart? Did it bring joy or pain because I hurt them while trying to get ahead in life?

_____
_____
_____
_____

After answering the questions above, read the prayer on the next page. Then open up your heart to grant access to the Father to remove every weed (sin) that is not like Him.

Father, right now,

I ask you to break all strongholds of fear, lack of trust,

and unforgiveness and any other associated fruit that has a tight hold or grip

on my life in Jesus' name. I ask you Father to restore my soul and my faith and begin to teach me to forgive others and then forgive myself. I ask you, Father, to help me to truly trust and show me how to rely on you and you alone. I ask you, Father, to help me learn and show love towards everyone just like you love me. I ask you, Father, to make my ways ultimately your ways. Transform my mind, body, and soul to do your will.

I pray this prayer to you, Father,

in the mighty name of Jesus.

Amen!!!

A Rose: The Layers in A Transformation Process

    Praying the prayer on the previous page will draw you one step closer to the Father. In the beginning, focusing on the Father will be hard, but the more you pray and read His Word, the easier it gets. Just stay focused and don't give up because deliverance will happen in God's timing, not ours. Always remember, God's Spirit dwells in us because we belong to Him. 1 John 4:4 (NKJV) says, "You are of God, little children, and have overcome them, because He who is in you is greater than he who is in the world."

Seed for Thought: The only way to rid weeds (sins) from your life is Jesus. Do you believe He is the only way to receive complete deliverance? If your answer is yes, then release and watch the Father give back ever stolen possession ever taken from you by Satan. Psalm 51:7-10 (NLT) says, "Purify me from my sins, and I will be clean; wash me, and I will be whiter than snow. Oh, give me back my joy again; you have broken me, now let me rejoice. Don't keep looking at my sins. Remove the stain of my guilt. Create in me a clean heart, O God. Renew a loyal spirit within me."

The only way to cast out all fears is to depend entirely on the Father.

One day, while sitting outside working on this book, as I have done on several occasions. I noticed several squirrels running around. Usually, I do not worry. This particular day, a squirrel developed boldness and courage to come near me. At first, I was calm until the squirrel got so close, I could physically touch it. The squirrel, while standing on his hind legs, looked me in the eyes, hoping I would be afraid or give some food. The longer it stayed, I became scared and decided to get up and run. After reaching the apartment, I stopped to look back. The squirrel was behind me. I picked up a rock to throw into the field to trick the squirrel into thinking I was throwing food. The squirrel still did not budge or move. Finally, a few minutes later, the squirrel went on its way.

Seed for Thought: Satan uses tactics to bombard the mind out of fear and doubt that God is not capable of removing an animal or a person from your life just by mentioning the name of Jesus. By saying that one precious name grants complete access over to the Father all of our hidden areas (secrets). What hidden areas (secrets) is Satan using against you to make you doubt God's abilities? (Psalms 139:23-24)

_____
_____
_____
_____
_____

By Wisdom A House Is

Built.

Through Knowledge Its Walls Are

Filled With Rare And

Beautiful Treasures.

Lock or Unlock the Hidden Areas (Secrets)

"No one, when he has lit a lamp, covers it with a vessel or puts it under a bed, but sets it on a lampstand, that those who enter may see the light. For nothing is secret that will not be revealed, nor anything hidden that will not be known and come to light."

Luke 8:16-17 (NKJV)

Fear is the main reason people keep hidden areas (secrets) locked away, so no one will see their true identity, especially if sin has manifested inside the heart. To completely grasp the understanding of bad qualities, refer back to Galatians 5:19-21. All hidden areas (secrets) are dangerous if not dealt with; they will surface, cause chaos, and leave a trail of broken hearts and promises. Satan uses those same hidden areas (secrets) as a distraction technique to get us not to focus on accomplishing God's plans. If any hidden areas (secrets) are left undisturbed, eventually, an individual will feel shame or guilt for any wrongful acts committed. For example, according to Genesis 3:7-11, God knew Adam and Eve ate from the tree of knowledge of good and evil before stepping foot inside the Garden of Eden. Adam and Eve heard God calling them, so they hid in the bushes feeling guilty and covering their naked bodies with fig leaves. According to Matthew 26:14-16, Jesus knew Judas would betray him for thirty pieces of silver. Judas felt ashamed that he betrayed Jesus, gave back the money, and hung himself. According to Luke 22:34, Jesus told Peter he would deny knowing Him three times before the rooster crowed. Peter realized his wrongdoing, felt guilty, and asked for forgiveness. Jeremiah 23:24 (NLT) says, "Can anyone hide from me in a secret place? Am I not everywhere in all the heavens and earth?" says the Lord.

Seed for Thought: God is everywhere and knows everything. Are you running and hiding from God? Do you not believe He is capable of handling all of your mess? Why? (Psalm 139:7-10)

_____

_____

_____

_____

_____

_____

_____

Being still is the only way to know the one true living God!

In the Old Testament, Jeremiah told the people they needed to turn away from sin by letting the Potter crush, remove, and reshape them into vessels He could use (Jeremiah 18:1-12). In the New Testament, Peter told the people, according to Acts 3:19-20 (NLT), "Now repent of your sins and turn to God, so that your sins may be wiped away. Then times of refreshment will come from the presence of the Lord, and he will again send you Jesus, your appointed Messiah". Even today, many ordained men and women of God are preaching the same message as Jeremiah and Peter to believe, repent, and submit their life entirely to Christ to inherit eternal life with the Father forever.

Seed for Thought: It may be humanly impossible to live a perfect life. Through obeying God's word, and allowing His spirit to direct our path, all things are possible. 2 Chronicles

7:14-15 (NLT) says "Then if my people who are called by my name will humble themselves and pray and seek my face and turn from their wicked ways, I will hear from heaven and will forgive their sins and restore their land. My eyes will be open and my ears attentive to every prayer made in this place" to grasp the understanding that …

A Rose: The Layers in A Transformation Process

    Erasing all locked areas allows God to cleanse the mind, body, and spirit from the prison of all hidden areas (secrets) to create a liberated and revitalized vessel free from sin. John 8:34-36 (NIV) says, "Jesus replied, Very truly I tell you, everyone who sins is a slave to sin. Now a slave has no permanent place in the family, but a son belongs to it forever. So, if the Son sets you free, you will be free indeed." Experiencing freedom through the hands of Jesus alters an individual's identity, lifestyle, and conversation, which makes an individual want to remain pure, loving, and compassionate toward others, and live their life according to God's plan without fear of people's opinions.

Seed for Thought: Freedom from bondage, freedom to live life without regrets, freedom to explore, dream, and achieve the impossible. Are you free by Christ's or man's standard? Why? (Galatians 5:1)

Removal of Weeds (Sins)

Our Heavenly Father is not in the business of judging our hidden areas (secrets) or exposing our weeds (sins) to the world as men do. 1 Samuel 16:7 (NIV) says, "The Lord does not look at the things people look at. People look at the outward appearance, but the Lord looks at the heart," that is intricate with hidden areas (secrets) of wickedness to uproot, discard, and remember no more (Hebrews 8:12). As the Father removes from the soul, all hidden areas (secrets), white and red rose seeds of purity, and love is replanted back into the vessel's newly cultivated spirit. Then the mind will think positive thoughts; the heart will release loving emotions and speak encouraging words to others. Out of the soul, seeds of life will spring forth and shine bright in the darkness. Proverb 17:22 (NLT) states, "A cheerful heart is good medicine, but a broken spirit saps a person's strength."

Seed for Thought: If Jesus was in the same room as you, would your light shine or blend in with the crowd in the room? Would He be proud or disappointed in your action? Why? (Matthew 5:16)

Personal Reflection

Chapter Three

Mulch - Seeds of Life

Life without direction leads to failure. Experience with guidance opens the door to success.

The seed of life was given back to humanity the day a Virgin named Mary conceived a child named Jesus. Everywhere He ministered the people heard, according to John 14:6 (NLT), "I am the way, the truth, and the life. No one can come to the Father except through me." And John 6:35 (NLT), "I am the bread of life. Whoever comes to me will never be hungry again. Whoever believes in me will never be thirsty." Jesus' ministry was top notch with no flaws, imperfections, or errors. His mercy gave everyone hope for a brighter future, grace to finish the race, and love to overcome the hatred faced every day. Never once did He whine or complain about being the Chosen vessel used to light a dark, sin tainted world.

Seed for Thought: Man does not choose God. God chose man with all their imperfections and flaws to continue lighting a dark, sin tainted world. Has God Chosen you? If yes, I challenge you to jot down on the space below, the many blessings God has given to you as a beautiful reminder that His love never fails (Ephesians 1:3-9).

_____

_____

_____

_____

_____

_____

_____

Jesus' primary purpose in life was to show servanthood by demonstrating the Fruit of Spirit qualities according to Galatians 5:22-23 (NIV) "But the fruit of the Spirit is love, joy, peace, longsuffering, kindness, goodness, faithfulness, gentleness, self-control. Against such, there is no law." His unconditional love for His Father kept Him driven to heal the blind, tell a lame man to walk, cure lepers, unstop deaf ears, and raise the dead while proclaiming the good news to the poor that God will provide every need and heal their bodies when sick (Matthew 11:4-5). Jesus demonstrated the Fruit of Spirit qualities through the many miracles performed while ministering to the people. As you read the stories about the Fruit of the Spirit Qualities, ask the Holy Spirit (Comforter) to unclog your ears to hear the Father's small still voice to clarify and envision Jesus performing nine out of the thirty-seven miracles administered in the Bible.

Fruit of the Spirit Qualities

A Seed of Love[5] happened when the Savior was born in a stable because no one would give Mary and Joseph a room. For thirty-three years, the Son of God walked on this earth in the form of a man preaching and teaching the word of God. While ministering, He showed love to a woman with an issue of blood. For twelve years, she dealt with this infirmity. Her strong faith in God caused her to believe, touching His cloak, would heal her. One day she became so desperate and determined to touch Jesus' cloak, she crawled under people to get to Him. Once she touched His cloak, Jesus looked around for the person who touched Him. After looking all around, He decided to look down. While looking down, He noticed a woman on the ground, immediately His heart filled with great compassion toward her. Jesus said daughter having great faith has made you whole. She quickly realized healing had taken place in her body (Matthew 9:20-21).

Seed for Thought: When a person becomes determined or desperate to rid weeds (sins) out of their life, no one or nothing can stand in the way of them being in the presence of the master. Are you desperate and ready for a change in your life? How will you make the change? (Psalms 147:3)

_____
_____
_____
_____
_____

A Seed of Joy[5] happened after Jesus raised Lazarus from the dead. Jesus loved Mary, Martha, and their brother Lazarus. While Jesus was ministering, He heard Lazarus was sick but did not leave the place He was ministering until two days later after Lazarus had died. While waiting for Jesus, Mary and Martha wrapped Lazarus' body with cloth and placed him in a tomb. Everyone was sad and disappointed at the same time. When Jesus finally arrived, He acknowledged to everyone that Lazarus was only sleeping, but everyone knew he was already dead. Jesus followed Mary and Martha to the tomb and asked the people to roll back the stone. While Jesus was waiting, He looked up into the sky and thanked the Father first for always hearing Him. Then Jesus told the Father. I did this for the benefit of the people who were standing here to believe that you sent me to earth to save the lost. Jesus spoke the words, Lazarus come forth and, immediately, he came out of the tomb, still wrapped in burial cloth (John 11:1-45).

Seed for Thought: Has God promised you anything, and it has not happened yet? If the answer is yes, be patient and remember everything happens in God's timing, not ours. Habakkuk 2:3 (NLT) says, "This vision is for a future time. It describes the end, and it will be fulfilled. If it seems slow in coming, wait patiently, for it will surely take place. It will not be delayed."

A Seed of Peace[5] happened when Jesus calmed the storm. Jesus got on the boat with the disciples. While He was sleeping, a bad storm arose. The disciples started panicking and woke Him up, saying, save us so that we won't drown. Jesus told the disciples; you have little faith and seem to be very afraid. At that very moment, He got up and rebuked the winds and waves which caused the sea to calm down. The disciples asked, who is this man that causes the winds and waves to obey? (Matthew 8:23-27; Mark 4:35-41; Luke 8:22-25)

Seed for Thought: Calling on the name of Jesus calms every storm, moves every mountain, and causes the devil to flee. When troubles arise, who do you call on to help fight your battles? (Deuteronomy 20:1,4)

_____

_____

_____

_____

A Seed of Patience[5] happened after Jesus healed a lame man who laid by the pool. There was a lame man disabled and confined to one area for thirty-eight years. Everyone around him was disabled and waiting patiently to get into the pool of Bethesda to receive healing. When Jesus saw the lame man, He asked him. Do you not want to be made whole? The lame man responded he has been waiting thirty-eight years for someone to help him get into the pool, and no one would help, or the people would go ahead of him. Jesus responded and said, a rise, take your mat and walk. The lame man received healing after thirty-eight years of laying by the pool of Bethesda (John 5:1-15).

Seed for Thought: We only discover our true identity and abilities while seeking and waiting patiently on the Lord so He can reveal the purpose that leads us into our destiny. Do you know your purpose in life? (Matthew 7:7)

_____

_____

_____

_____

A Seed of Kindness[5] happened the day Jesus turned water into wine at the wedding in Cana. The guest list included Jesus, his mother, the twelve disciples, and many others. By the third day of the celebration, there was no more wine. Jesus' mother looked at Him and said there is no more wine. Jesus responded, lady, why do you involve me? His mother ignored the comment and told the servants to listen to His instruction. Out of obedience, Jesus instructed the servants to collect six- 20 to 30-gallon stone water jars and fill them up with water. After all the jars were full of water, Jesus said to take the wine to the master of the house table so he can taste and approve. The master tasted the wine and looked at the bridegroom and said, bring out the choice wine first before serving the cheaper wine. Then the guest will have more to drink, leaving the best for last. Little did the master know, Jesus had transformed regular water into wine that was tastier and better quality than homegrown wine produced from grapes. The wedding in Cana was the first of many joyous occasions where Jesus revealed to the disciples that He was the Son of God (John 2:1-11).

Seed for Thought: Jesus decided to humble Himself and take no credit for turning water into wine but allowed the master of the house to receive all the glory, honor, and praise from the bridegroom. Is there ever a time in your life where you had to humble yourself so someone else could get the recognition you deserve? How did it make you feel? How did you handle everything? Did you demonstrate Christ-like qualities? (Proverbs 11:2)

_____
_____
_____
_____

A Seed of Goodness[5] happened after the servant of the high priest's ear was cut off. While Jesus was ministering to the crowd, Judas approached and kissed Him on the cheek. Jesus said to Judas, Are you the one who is betraying the Son of Man with a kiss on the cheek? When the followers saw the kiss, an altercation started. Everyone pulled out their sword to fight. While fighting, the servant of the high priest's ear was cut off. Jesus raised His voice and told the people to stop. He bent over and picked up the servant of the high priest's ear and reattached it to his head. Then Jesus turned and spoke to the Chief Priests, the officers of the temple guard, and the elders. Am I the one you are coming to kill? Do you believe in your heart I am leading a rebellion? Every day you saw me in the temple courts, and no one ever laid a hand on me. But today, this hour, darkness has decided to reign (Luke 22:47-53).

Seed for Thought: We must all strive to be compassionate towards one another. When we see a brother or sister in need, help them the way Christ has helped us. Luke 6:31 (NLT) says, "Do to others as you would like them to do to you." 1 Peter 3:8 (NLT) says, "Finally, all of you should be of one mind. Sympathize with each other. Love each other as brothers and sisters. Be tenderhearted and keep a humble attitude."

A Seed of Gentleness[5] happened after Jesus decided to wash the disciples' feet. The Passover Festival was about to start when the twelve disciples and Jesus sat down to break bread with one another. Satan had already planted a seed of deception in Judas' ear to betray Jesus. Jesus knew His time on earth was coming to an end. After eating, Jesus got up, took off His outer garment and wrapped a towel around His waist, and then poured water into a basin before washing and drying each of the disciple's feet. The only person who wanted special treatment was Simon Peter, who asked the master to cleanse his whole body. Jesus responded, if anyone has already cleansed their body, the only thing I need to do is wash their feet. Jesus said to the disciples, unless I am the one who cleanses your feet, you will not have any part of me. When Jesus finished washing everyone's feet, He put back on the outer garment and returned to his seat.

Jesus then asked the twelve disciples. Do you know what I have demonstrated to you? He continued telling them, calling me Teacher or Lord is correct, for that is who I truly am. Now that I am, your Teacher and Lord, and have washed your feet. Now it is time for you to wash one another's feet. I have demonstrated examples of servanthood. This is what I expect from you when showing love toward others. Always remember as you serve others that you are no more significant than your master, and neither is the messenger more excellent than the individual who sent the servant. Now that you know what to do, you will be blessed if you serve others over yourself (John 13:1-17).

Seed for Thought: Jesus chose to wash the disciple's feet to prove the master was no better than the servant. We are an imitator of Christ, called to serve others over self. Have you helped your neighbors today? What are some of the ways to serve your neighbors? (Mark 10:42-45)

_____
_____
_____
_____
_____
_____
_____

A Seed of Self-Control[5] happened after Jesus finished fasting for forty days and forty nights. He was tempted by Satan three different times. The first test was after Jesus finished fasting and was extremely hungry. Satan told Jesus, if you renounce being the Son of God, the stones will turn into bread. Jesus' response was. Man shall not live on bread alone but every word that comes from God. The second test was when Satan took Jesus to the Holy City and placed Him at the highest point of the temple. Satan said to Him again, if you say you are the Son of God, throw yourself off the temple and command the angels to rescue you so your feet will not touch the ground. Jesus' answered again; do not test the Lord thy God. The final test happened when Satan took Jesus to the tallest mountain and showed Him the world. Afterward, Satan said, bow down and worship me, and I will give you your heart's desires. Jesus' final response was. Satan gets thee behind me. I only praise and serve the one true living God. Satan left, and angels appeared to take care of Jesus (Matthew 4:1-11).

Seed for Thought: Jesus relied on His Heavenly Father to give Him strength during moments of weakness. In what area of your life are you weak? Do you fight temptation with the word of God or with your own words? (2 Corinthians 12: 9-10)

_____
_____
_____
_____
_____
_____
_____

A Seed of Faithfulness[5] happened after Jesus decided to obey His Heavenly Father and die on the cross. Jesus was captured and taken to the Governor's house for the trial of a crime He never committed. While Pilate was cross-examining Jesus, he asked Him, Do you believe you're the King of the Jews? Jesus replied, if that is what you believe, I agree. While remaining silent to all other accusations. Pilate knew at that very moment, Jesus was innocent and decided not to crucify him. Instead, He took out a basin filled with water, washed his hands in front of the crowd, and said, I will have no part of this innocent man's blood; it is now the people's responsibility. The crowd responded and said Jesus' blood would be on us and all of our children. While shouting louder and louder to release Barabbas and crucify Jesus (Matthew 27:11-26; 32-44).

Seed for Thought: An innocent man hung, bled, and died on the cross for a crime He never committed. The only crime Jesus committed was loving a sinful world unconditionally. Proverbs 17:17 (NKJV) says, "A friend loves at all times," because God commands us to "Love one another" as Christ loved us, so we must love each other (John 13:34).

Love suffered the pounding of nails driven into His hands and feet after being placed on a wooden cross for all sin, bondage, depression, rejection, low self-esteem, fear, lack of trust, unforgiveness, and any other associated fruit. A cross that absorbed the blood from Jesus' pierced, beaten and naked body. His resurrection extended life through the hand of mercy, so grace could draw us back to the same cross that could not sustain the Seed of Life. Love still tries to teach a tainted world self-control, peace, patience, and give joy while maintaining a pure and holy standard in the middle of muddy water.

Seeds of Life

Chapter Four

Water- Seasons

"For everything there is a season, a time for every activity under heaven."
Ecclesiastes 3:1 (NLT)

Our Heavenly Father knew the day His Son sacrificed His life on the cross; transformed vessels, cleansed by the blood of Jesus, would need help finishing their kingdom assignment. An advocate, in the form of the Holy Spirit (Comforter), would be sent to assist all transformed vessels from growing weary and desiring to go back to Egypt. The Holy Spirit's responsibilities include watering the converted vessel's minds with spiritual guidance, power, love, and encouragement during difficult seasons. Other assigned duties include drawing lost souls back to the cross, where they once nailed Jesus' body. Each individual would go through a cleansing process to remove all the black rose seeds of weeds (sins), before healthy white and red rose seeds of purity and love are embedded back into a clean vessel's spirit. The purpose of the cleansing process is to repair and rebuild the wounded vessel's spirit so dormant spiritual gifts planted deep within, can spring forth and lead the vessel into their destiny. Isaiah 58:11 (NLT) says, "The Lord will guide you continually, giving you water when you are dry and restoring your strength. You will be like a well-watered garden, like an ever-flowing spring."

Seed for Thought: Seasons are defining moments God uses to develop our inner character so the world will see our true identity. Jeremiah 1:5 (NIV) says, "Before I formed you in the womb, I knew you, before you were born, I set you apart; I appointed you as a prophet to the nations." Being separate from the world requires God to reveal the many seasons of our lives. Knowing helps us handle the season. Do you know...

What season are you experiencing right now?

A Rose: The Layers in A Transformation Process

Figure 1: Happy and Full of Life

Figure 2: Floating above the Clouds

45

Figure 3: Confused and In a Daze

Figure 4: Feeling Complacent

A Rose: The Layers in A Transformation Process

Figure 5: Down in the Dumps but a Glimpse of Hope

Figure 6: Optimistic for the Future

We can only assume the season we are experiencing, but God truly knows the answer. In due time everything will be revealed if we are still and seek Him in prayer. 2 Corinthians 4:16-18 (NLT) says, "That is why we never give up. Though our bodies are dying, our spirits are being renewed every day. For our present troubles are small and won't last very long. Yet they produce for us a glory that vastly outweighs them and will last forever! So, we don't look at the troubles we can see now; rather, we fix our gaze on things that cannot be seen. For the things we see now will soon be gone, but the things we cannot see will last forever." The only thing that matters the most in any season is to trust and lean on God for strength and guidance regardless if one minute we are floating above the clouds or experiencing a down in the dump moment. Always remember to look up toward Heaven and smile instead of looking down with a frown to realize God is in charge, and through Him, we can be optimistic about our future.

Seed for Thought: Embracing life without guidance is a challenge, but with guidance, all challenges faced will be fulfilling and rewarding if we don't give up. Who is guiding you to make your life fulfilling and rewarding? (Psalms 32:8)

_____
_____
_____
_____
_____
_____

A Rose: The Layers in A Transformation Process

In the bible, there was a man by the name of Saul. His profession was persecuting Christians before being converted to a Jesus follower on the road to Damascus (Acts 9). God altered Saul's character; Christian believers changed Saul's name to the Apostle Paul to fit his new spiritual identity (Acts 13:9). Apostle Paul suffered many seasons of trials and tribulations during his walk with God. He was beaten, stoned, placed in prison, and plotted against to kill by so-called believers for selfish reasons (Acts 19). He and other like-minded believers had to fight many battles with wisdom and the word of God. But through every adversity faced, God was there to guide, pick up, dust off, and restore their faith while giving Apostle Paul enough strength to endure in chains to the end. James 1:2-4 (NKJV) says it best, "My brethren, count it all joy when you fall into various trials, knowing that the testing of your faith produces patience. But let patience have its perfect work, that you may be perfect and complete, lacking nothing."

Seed for Thought: Anything worth working for never comes easy. Proverbs 16:9 (NIV), "In their hearts humans plan their course, but the Lord establishes their steps."

To succeed in life, we must all experience four seasonal stages; to grasp knowledge and understanding why God chose us, and the way He instructed the four seasons to come forth at the appropriate time. God spoke to fall to create cooler weather, colorful trees, and leaves before falling back to winter to cover up and protect everything until spring decides to come forward and reveal the true beauty that God hid before unveiling nature again through rays of sunshine and love in the summer. Isaiah 40:6-8 (NIV) tells us, "All people are like grass, and all their faithfulness is like the flowers of the field. The grass withers and the flowers fall, because the breath of the Lord blows on them. Surely the people are grass. The grass withers and the flowers fall, but the word of our God endures forever."

Seed for Thought: Putting our faith and trust in God gives us the wisdom to stand for truth and righteousness when Satan is trying to destroy us. Proverbs 2:9-15 (NIV) says, "Then you will understand what is right and just and fair—every good path. For wisdom will enter your heart, and knowledge will be pleasant to your soul. Discretion will protect you, and understanding will guard you. Wisdom will save you from the ways of wicked men, from men whose words are perverse, who have left the straight paths to walk in dark ways, who delight in doing wrong and rejoice in the perverseness of evil, whose paths are crooked and who are devious in their ways." Vessels, who's instructing you during the Four Seasonal Stages of your life to receive complete deliverance and transformation into a Chosen vessel?

Four Seasonal Stages

    Throughout life, we all experience obstacles that try our character and strengthen our faith. The ability to see beyond those obstacles make it hard to grasp an understanding of why everything is falling apart. Satan uses our mind, weakness, people, and objects to convince us that God does not love us, especially when life takes a turn for the worse that is unexpected and unplanned. The unexplainable event causes the mind to relapse and remember other moments of letdowns or mistakes which trigger fear and other negative emotions that blame others, ask why and doubt God's existence; to justify reasoning why life is collapsing before our eyes. Even the Children of Israel responded harshly by blaming God and other people for being stuck in the wilderness. After Moses told them, "Don't be afraid. Stand firm and watch God do His work of salvation for you today"(Exodus 14:13 MSG). Vessels, staying strong through adversity shows Satan our faith is in God, not our situation, people, or abilities. To fully experience God's unconditional love, we must go through what I call the Four Seasonal Stages. These four stages allow you to be torn down, built back up, and sharpened to do His mighty work, just like Apostle Paul. 2 Corinthians 4:7-9 (NKJV) says, "But we have this treasure in earthen vessels, that the excellence of the power may be of God and not of us. We are hard-pressed on every side, yet not crushed; we are perplexed, but not in despair; persecuted, but not forsaken; struck down, but not destroyed."

When despair happens, we are in Seasonal Stage One called **Devastation.** During this stage, our negative emotions only visualize the color red out of anger and rage. Devastation includes feelings of being abandoned, trapped, alone, confused, and betrayed by the people who say they love us, especially God. In our mind, we rehearse all scenarios over and over while trying to find answers to the why questions. Such as....

- Why did I get laid off from my job?
- Why did I get a divorce or end a long-term relationship?
- Why did the bank foreclose on my house, or my car gets repossessed?
- Why am I struggling financially when everyone else seems to be doing better than me?

- Why is my life_____ (fill in the blank with your questions)?

Asking why questions can go on and on until hearing the desired answer that satisfies the flesh. What happens if we never receive the answers to all our Why questions? Do we start playing the victim role for sympathy or remain in denial forever, or do we release everything to the Father to help us figure out why our situations or circumstances went in the wrong direction? According to Apostle Paul in 2 Corinthians 12:10 (NLT), "That's why I take pleasure in my weaknesses, and in the insults, hardships, persecutions, and troubles that I suffer for Christ. For when I am weak, then I am strong." Yes, even Apostle Paul struggled with weakness, but his strength and peace came from God, not flesh, to endure every obstacle faced. We, too, have the same advantage as Apostle Paul; His name is Jesus Christ. Hebrews 12:1-4 (NLT) says, "Therefore, since we are surrounded by such a huge crowd of witnesses to the life of faith, let us strip off every weight that slows us down, especially the sin that so easily trips us up. And let us run with endurance the race God has set before us. We do this by keeping our eyes on Jesus, the champion who initiates and perfects our faith. Because of the joy awaiting him, he endured the cross, disregarding its shame. Now he is seated in the place of honor beside God's throne. Think of all the hostility he endured from sinful people; then you won't become weary and give up. After all, you have not yet given your lives in your struggle against sin." If God is not allowed an opportunity to interrupt our thinking process, eventually, Satan will control our minds completely. Every vessel must become aware of the deceptive tactics Satan uses to hinder our walk with God.

Seed for Thought: In life, we all face many adversities, but the only way to pass with flying colors is to turn our focus off of I and place our eyes on Him. As we begin to realize, we are not alone and start to grasp understanding during the Devastation Stage; God's love in the form of sunshine rays will visibly appear through the walls of confusion as a sign of hope to tell us, "We know that we are children of God, and that the whole world is under the control of the evil one"(1 John 5:19 (NIV). Why do you think the letter "I" is in the middle of the word HIM? (Psalm 33:22)

_____

_____

_____

_____

_____

_____

_____

As a child of God, all vessels must allow the Holy Spirit (Comforter) to transition their mind to Seasonal Stage Two, which is called **Justification**. During this stage, the vessel's mind is trying to think of ways to remain angry for the situation that placed them into Devastation. As time passes, confusion, uncertainty, and negative emotions such as anger or rage begin to subside. Making it easy for God's rays of love to penetrate through the walls of deception to hear His voice tell us: Trust Me, I Got You! Just keep walking by faith regardless of what we see ahead (2 Corinthians 5:7). Trusting God teaches us how to differentiate between what is the truth and what is a lie, so Devastation and Justification won't be able to continue reaping havoc in our life. Proverbs 3:7-8 (NLT) says, "Don't be impressed with your own wisdom. Instead, fear the Lord and turn away from evil. Then you will have healing for your body and strength for your bones."

Seed for Thought: Healing restores peace to the mind, energy to the body, and tranquility to the soul. Psalms 147:3 (NIV) says, "He heals the brokenhearted and binds up their wounds." Vessels, when was the last time you spoke intimately with the Father? Stop right now and say the prayer below to begin the healing process.

"Our Father

which art in heaven, Hallowed be

thy name. Thy kingdom come, thy will be done

in earth, as it is in heaven. Give us this day our daily

bread. And forgive us our debts, as we forgive our debtors.

And lead us not into temptation, but deliver us from evil:

For thine is the kingdom, and the power, and the glory,

forever Amen. "

Matthew 6:9-13 (KJV)

The prayer on the previous page teaches us about forgiveness and what we should do concerning other people. Not forgiving stops the overflow of blessings released into our lives and allows people to have control over us. Matthew 6:14-15 (NIV) says, "For if you forgive other people when they sin against you, your heavenly Father will also forgive you. But if you do not forgive others their sins, your Father will not forgive your sins." Forgiving and repenting for our sins, draws us closer to the Father through continual teaching and conditioning the mind, body, and soul to submit to the Father's will.

When the vessels are ready, God will allow the Holy Spirit (Comforter) to transition them to Seasonal Stage Three called **Acceptance**. During this stage, the vessels are healing and starting to see their future through the eyes of God. The vessels only see a bright clear, straight, and narrow pathway with options to choose right or left. Going down the right path enhances the vessel's spiritual mindset to see life moving forward, not backward, with an optimistic attitude about their future. Going down the left pathway (wrong) makes it easy for Satan to continue disclosing our past to the world as free cheap entertainment with unlimited movie passes for lifetime previews. 1 John 4:4-6 (NKJV) says, "You are of God, little children, and have overcome them, because He who is in you is greater than he who is in the world. They are of the world. Therefore, they speak *as* of the world, and the world hears them. We are of God. He who knows God hears us; he who is not of God does not hear us. By this we know the Spirit of truth and the Spirit of error."

Seed for Thought: The Spirit of truth teaches us to accept life with no regrets (Proverbs 9:9-10), not to dwell but reflect on the past (Isaiah 43:18-19), so God can change what needs to be changed, to create the best version of you. 2 Corinthians 5:17 (NKJV) says, "Therefore, if anyone is in Christ, he *is* a new creation; old things have passed away; behold, all things have become new."

Yielding our will helps to transition vessels into Seasonal Stage Four called **Surrendering**. During this stage, God has complete access to our body, mind, and spirit to use as instruments to bring back home other vessels that have gone astray. He also enhances the vessel's memory to dream and achieve the impossible. By staying connected spiritually, God opens the windows of opportunity to spread His word, be a good Christian role model to everyone we meet while maintaining a positive attitude with a smile on their face, especially on emotional days. Ephesians 5:1-2 (NIV) says, "Follow God's example, therefore, as dearly loved children and walk in the way of love, just as Christ loved us and gave himself up for us as a fragrant offering and sacrifice to God."

Seed for Thought: Surrendering our will is easy to accept when the pathway is sunny and bright. Not as easy to release when clouds of Devastation and Justification are hanging over our heads. How do you handle those cloudy, gloomy days?

_____

_____

_____

_____

Praise God with a dance the way David did when the trumpet blew as the Ark of God was brought back home to Jerusalem (2 Samuel 6:14-15). I challenge everyone to put a smile on their face, praise in their step, and say out loud - I am not a negative nobody, but **A Successful Somebody** who is "fearfully and wonderfully made" by God (Psalms 139:14). Eventually, in God's timing, all vessels will transform into Chosen vessels. Who sees themselves as God's true beauty evolving into Noble Men of Valor or Beautiful Butterflies[6]; that is capable of seeing themselves soar above cloudy, gloomy days of adversity.

Personal Reflection

_____

_____

_____

_____

_____

_____

Chapter Five

Inspections - Admiring the Beauty

"But you are a chosen generation, a royal priesthood, a holy nation, His own special people, that you may proclaim the praises of Him who called you out of darkness into His marvelous light; who once were not a people but are now the people of God, who had not obtained mercy but now have obtained mercy." 1 Peter 2:9-10 (NKJV)

Now that the Chosen vessel has surrendered every aspect of their life over to the Father to carry out their purpose, a protective veil or covering is immediately placed over them to protect against Satan and all his followers who desire to attack the Chosen vessel. Psalm 34:19 (NLT) says, "The righteous person faces many troubles, but the Lord comes to the rescue each time." God even protects us from ourselves. We're our own worst enemy, especially when our spirit is weak. We give in to the weakness of our flesh like a fly that becomes intrigued by a spider's web right before being captured.

2 Corinthians 12:9 (NIV) says, "My grace is sufficient for you, for my power is made perfect in weakness." To prevent yielding to our flesh, we must pray and cleave to the Father for protection and strength until the spiritual attack is over. Chosen vessels, the Father, is well aware and will shield us every time we call His name. Psalm 57:1-3 (NIV) says, "Have mercy on me, my God, have mercy on me, for in you I take refuge. I will take refuge in the shadow of your wings until the disaster has passed. I cry out to God Most High, to God, who vindicates me. He sends from heaven and saves me, rebuking those who hotly pursue me, God sends forth his love and his faithfulness." As long as every Chosen vessel focuses on the Father, He promises, according to Psalm 121:1-8 (NIV), "I lift up my eyes to the mountains, where does my help come from? My help comes from the Lord, the Maker of heaven and earth. He will not let your foot slip, he who watches over you will not slumber; indeed, he who watches over Israel will neither slumber nor sleep. The Lord watches over you, the Lord is your shade at your right hand; the sun will not harm you by day, nor the moon by night. The Lord will keep you from all harm, he will watch over your life; the Lord will watch over your coming and going both now and forevermore." Even when we do not deserve to be loved or protected, God still loves us unconditionally.

Seed for Thought: When God's love surrounds us nothing, or nobody can penetrate His powerful shield of protection. Chosen vessels, whose love surrounds you daily? (Job 11:17-19) Stop right now and read Psalm 91. After reading, ask the Holy Spirit (Comforter) to refresh your memory to remember every way God extends protection and blessings to you daily. Then jot down each memory and say "Thank You" as a sign of gratitude and appreciation to the Father for His love bestowed to us daily (Psalm 100:4-5).

_____

_____

_____

_____

_____

_____

_____

Not only does the Father provide continuous protection, but He also guarantees all Chosen vessels will flourish if they follow the plans already laid out for them. His way includes daily prayer (Psalm 66:17), the word of God (Psalm 143:5-6), and other essential materials needed for spiritual growth. Growth includes inspirational books, listening to encouraging music, going to Christian conferences, and serving in a spirit-filled Biblical Church while taking yearly sabbatical trips to renew and recharge the inner spirit. Even

Jesus, while walking on Earth, took sabbatical trips to fast and pray for the strength to finish His assignment, before giving up the ghost to be with His Father forever. Chosen vessels, there were six different occasions when Jesus needed solitude to seek wisdom from the Father concerning:

1. A significant task before finishing His assignment– Luke 4: 1-2, 14-15
2. Guidance- Luke 5:16
3. Making an important decision – Luke 6:12-13
4. Distress (troubled)- Luke 22:39-44
5. Grief- Matthew 14:1-13
6. Refreshing and recharging – Mark 6:30-32

Jesus' only desire was pleasing His Father. We, as modern-day Chosen vessels, must desire to please the Father more than self. We must strive to finish our course to receive a crown of righteousness with benefits that include spending eternity with the Father. Proverbs 2:1-5 (NLT) says, "My child, listen to what I say, and treasure my commands. Tune your ears to wisdom and concentrate on understanding. Cry out for insight and ask for understanding. Search for them as you would for silver; seek them like hidden treasures. Then you will understand what it means to fear the Lord, and you will gain knowledge of God."

Seed for Thought: Wisdom changes our perspective, gives us strength, guides, and protects us on our spiritual journey. Romans 15:4-6 (NIV) says, "For everything that was written in the past was written to teach us, so that through the endurance taught in the Scriptures and the encouragement they provide we might have hope. May the God who gives endurance and encouragement give you the same attitude of mind toward each other that Christ Jesus had, so that with one mind and one voice you may glorify the God and Father of our Lord Jesus Christ." Stop right now and say the simple prayer on the next page for wisdom, strength, and the ability to see yourself as a Chosen vessel eventually transformed into a Noble Man of Valor or a Beautiful Butterfly.

Father right now, I humbly come again wounded and broken asking for you to forgive me, and take away all my sins that I have allowed to creep back into my life. Forgive me for every time I heard your voice and ignored it to do my own selfish will instead of your will. I ask you to come into my mind, heart, and soul to purify and cleanse me from the crown of my head to the soles of my feet. Renew, transform, and realign every area of my life to line up with your will. Search every crevice inside my body, removing any weeds (sins) that separate me from you. I ask you to help me to continue seeing myself as your Chosen vessel, so I can do your will and guarantee my name is written in the book of life forever. I thank you Father for not giving up on me. I thank you again for the wonderful privileges given. In Jesus Christ Name I pray. Amen!

Through every generation of Chosen vessels, God has inspected their beauty while on the Potter's wheel, making sure the Noble Men of Valor or Beautiful Butterflies are ready for their call to duty. These are the elite men and women who have earned the right to lead and guide other vessels into their destiny. The elite Chosen vessels are faithful individuals who love serving others over self without expecting any reward. 2 Corinthians 1:21-22 (NLT) says, "It is God who enables us, along with you, to stand firm for Christ. He has commissioned us, and he has identified us as his own by placing the Holy Spirit in our hearts as the first installment that guarantees everything he has promised us." God sees all

His creations as elite Chosen vessels, capable of living life to the fullest while walking into their destiny. The problem is not God but us.

We make up every excuse not to serve God, such as life is too hectic, infirmities (weakness), financial struggles, age, job, lack of experience, or children until a handout is needed, then we serve God with all our heart. In Acts 3:1-10, a lame man laid at the temple gates called Beautiful. Everyday people would carry and place him by the gates to beg for money. His deformities were the excuse needed to look down on life until Peter and John asked him to look up and focus on them. Peter immediately said to the lame man I do not have any silver or gold, but what I do have I am delighted to give to you. Peter said in the name of Jesus Christ, get up and walk. Immediately his deformities were replaced with beauty, strength to walk, a joy to leap, and praises for healing.

Seed for Thought: What excuses have you used as a crutch to not serve God or fulfill your purpose? (Ezekiel 36:25-27) Chosen vessels, God did not create anyone to sit on the sidelines as a negative nobody but **A Successful Somebody** who's designed to make a difference in this world.

_____
_____
_____
_____
_____
_____
_____

I am not a negative nobody

but

A Successful SOMEBODY!

"Now then, we are ambassadors for Christ, as though God were pleading through us: we implore you on Christ's behalf, be reconciled to God. 21 For He made Him who knew no sin to be sin for us, that we might become the righteousness of God in Him."

2 Corinthians 5:20-21 (NKJV)

We all, from time to time, have felt like a negative nobody while allowing the mind to wander or sometimes ponder about going back to Egypt with the occasional moments of asking the why questions discussed in Chapter Four. The only possible answer is familiarity. Familiarity makes it easy to become stagnant or content with the same daily routine while choosing the same type of intimate relationship. The lame man at the gate of Beautiful was familiar with the same daily routine until Peter and John altered his plans. Familiarity clouds the mind into believing the quality of life is better in Egypt instead of seeking, praying, and fasting to the Father to keep moving forward. Egypt does not always have to be a physical location but a person or a particular lifestyle. Egypt can be a combination of all three, which causes the mind to feel trapped without an escape route to freedom. 1 Corinthians 10:13 (NIV) states, "No temptation has overtaken you except what is common to mankind. And God is faithful; he will not let you be tempted beyond what you can bear. But when you are tempted, he will also provide a way out so that you can endure it."

Seed for Thought: God's love accepts us as we are before transforming us into righteous men and women of God. Hebrews 12:11 (NLT) says, "No discipline is enjoyable while it is happening—it's painful! But afterward, there will be a peaceful harvest of right living for those who are trained in this way."

Did you know that the caterpillar species must go through a metamorphosis cycle before transforming into a beautiful magnificent colorful butterfly that captivates the human eye? The beginning cycle always starts with the female butterfly searching for the appropriate location to lay her eggs. After finding the perfect place to lay an egg, the caterpillar is born. The caterpillar's primary job is to eat until it is big enough to reproduce new skin that covers the entire body. This cycle is called Chrysalis. The caterpillar will remain in the state of Chrysalis until it becomes strong enough to break away the thick protective shell to reveal to the world an adult butterfly created by God. Similar to the caterpillar, our external hard layers of weeds (sins) that cover the internal core of our spirit are removed first before God's love can shine from inside out.

BEAUTY is not seen or touched; it is felt through LOVE!

To strive towards genuine love, man must grant complete access to their heart to God. There will be times everyone will struggle granting access to their heart to God, due to being blinded by the world to see beyond the false mirror image of the world to envision a bright, prosperous future. The adversary of this world has paralyzed our minds to see mistakes, failures, hurts, and disappointment caused by other people. We start to view ourselves as a negative nobody not capable of living a blessed life (2 Corinthians 4:4). When a person is a negative nobody with a pessimist spirit, they will always complain and judge others instead of seeing their faults (Matthew 7:3-5). These individuals love playing the victim role in every situation instead of recognizing their destructive tongue is victimizing others (James 3:1-12). These individuals are defensive, self-centered, and never want to hear the truth. To break the generational curse of a negative nobody man must allow God complete access to their soul. Romans 8:6 (NIV), "The mind governed by the flesh is death, but the mind governed by the Spirit is life and peace." King Saul demonstrated qualities of a negative nobody, especially after God removed His mirror image of true beauty from him and placed it on the inside of David while he was playing the harp (1 Samuel 16:14-23).

Seed for Thought: True beauty represents the attributes that makeup God's heart. What characteristics should we all strive to possess after being transformed and renewed by the blood of Jesus?

_____

_____

_____

_____

_____

_____

After reading the verses below, on the space provided, write **ONE** word from each scripture that describes an attribute of God. The answers are in the Appendix section of the book[7].

A. Deuteronomy 5:33 _____

B. Luke 6:37 _____

C. Philippians 4:5 _____

D. Proverbs 15:29 _____

E. Proverbs 22:21 _____

F. Proverbs 25:28 _____

G. Psalm 25:9 _____

H. Psalm 40:1 _____

I. Psalm 103:13 _____

J. Romans 13:10 _____

David was an elite Chosen vessel used by God according to Acts 13:22 (NIV), which says, "After removing Saul, he made David their king. God testified concerning him: I have found David son of Jesse, a man after my own heart; he will do everything I want him to do." David demonstrated qualities of humility, respect, trust, faith, love, and obedience with a sincere heart of repentance after sinning. 1 Corinthians 6:17 (NLT) says. "But the person who is joined to the Lord is one spirit with him." All Chosen vessels who possess a true beauty's heart can see themselves as **A Successful Somebody** with an optimist spirit; striving to mimic God's mirror image of perfection (Matthew 5:48), not ashamed of the gospel (Roman 1:16), bold and confident like Peter, and speak the truth like Paul. These individuals will always light up a room with their unique personality while ministering encouraging words to everyone they meet (Philippians 2:5). God's word tells us that "Gracious words are a honeycomb, sweet to the soul and healing to the bones (Proverbs 16:24)." **A Successful Somebody** never dwells about Egypt but only reflects while learning from their mistakes, failures, hurts, and disappointment made so, the past will not carry over into their future. A future that will shine bright, if the individual always trusts, believes, and stays focused on the Father so His peace can sustain them on the mountain top and protect them in the valley. Psalm 23 (NIV) says, "The Lord is my shepherd, I lack nothing. He makes me lie down in green pastures, he leads me beside quiet waters, he refreshes my soul. He guides me along the right paths for his name's sake. Even though I walk through the darkest valley, I will fear no evil, for you are with me; your rod and your staff, they comfort me. You prepare a table before me in the presence of my enemies. You anoint my head with oil; my cup overflows. Surely your goodness and love will follow me all the days of my life, and I will dwell in the house of the Lord forever." Always remember, trials don't come to destroy anyone but to make them stronger. If we don't give up, we are capable of being the Chosen vessels God intended for us to be. Everything in life happens on God's timing and not a moment sooner. While waiting, continue letting the Father prune, poke, and pull all weeds (sins) out of us, so we can become God's priceless gift to the world.

Seed for Thought: Chosen vessels, each day we open our eyes, take a deep breath, and see the blue blood flowing through our veins proves God still loves us unconditionally. We are His children, and now is the time we should take a serious look at ourselves in the mirror while answering the following questions. Do I display the image of a negative nobody with a pessimistic spirit or **A Successful Somebody** with an optimistic spirit who is not afraid to let true beauty shine forever? _____

Poem

TRUE BEAUTY is not what we see in a magazine, movie, or television. True Beauty is not about our size or the measurements we used to fit in. True Beauty is not the clothes we wear, the haircut or hairstyle, or the makeup worn to cover up flaws and imperfections like concealer, so the world thinks we have it all together. True Beauty is not the people we hang around, our job, the men and women who whistle, smile, or say they are interested in you, which may or may not be real. BUT... True Beauty is God, who sacrificed His life on the cross for us so we can become Noble Men of Valor or Beautiful Butterflies. God created us to use our size, unique style, and colorful personality to relight the burnt-out candle, so God's glory can shine brightly in a dark, sinful world again. That's …

True Beauty!!

Admiring the Beauty

Chapter Six

Prune- Priceless

"The fear of the Lord is the beginning of knowledge, But fools despise wisdom and instruction."
Proverbs 1:7 (NKJV)

As winter began to vanish and spring appeared, I decided to take a walk outside to get some fresh air and clear my head. At the beginning of the walk, my mind and body were saying no, but my spirit was saying yes to the Father. Matthew 26:41 (NLT) says, "Keep watch and pray, so that you will not give in to temptation. For the spirit is willing, but the body is weak!" This particular path was very familiar; except this time, the Father decided to heighten my spiritual eyes over my natural eyes to reveal several beautiful purple flowers blooming on leafless tree branches.

While admiring the beautiful purple flowers, I could hear the birds chirping and the geese quacking loudly. It was as if creation was praising and worshipping the one true living God, who created everything during the breaking ground (Chapter One). Luke 19:40 (NIV) says, "If we keep silent and do not praise and worship Him the rocks will cry out letting the world know that He is still alive, in control and deserves to be praised." As I continued walking, I noticed a man and a woman feeding a bunch of wild geese. I instantly became intrigued and blown away at how trustworthy both species were toward each other, considering at any given moment, both species could turn on each other.

Seed for Thought: What do you think would happen if the man decided to lift his hands towards the creator instead of putting his hands down to feed creation, especially since the creator created creation? (Psalm 116:1-2)

A Rose: The Layers in A Transformation Process

_____
_____
_____
_____

After observing the interactions between both species, I continued walking until reaching a small reddish-brown wooden bridge. I immediately noticed approximately 15 to 20 locks with names written on them while hanging on a black wire that was attached to the bridge. Like I stated earlier, this was not a usual leisure walk but a walk with the creator to let me know He still reigns and rules in the universe regardless if we choose not to believe He indeed exists. Hebrews 1:10-12 (NLT) says, "In the beginning, Lord, you laid the foundation of the earth and made the heavens with your hands. They will perish, but you remain forever. They will wear out like old clothing. You will fold them up like a cloak and discard them like old clothing. But you are always the same; you will live forever."

For many years men and women have always found different ways to express their unconditional love for one another. A love lock or padlock love is just one-way couples show their love toward each other by writing both names on a lock before attaching the lock to a bridge forever. Our Heavenly Father expressed true love when He sent His one and only son down from Heaven to be born in a womb, to preach and teach the gospel before commanding Jesus to sacrifice His life on the cross. True love hung, bled, died, and rose again for a sinful world that believes genuine love written on locks that are attached to a wire on a wooden bridge that eventually gets cut off by men represent real love. The Father guarantees to Love you like a brother (Proverbs 18:24), never leave you nor forsake you when times get tough (Deuteronomy 31:6). When you ask, He will provide wisdom and understanding concerning any area of your life (Song of Solomon 8:6-7). The God I serve will never waver, distort, or provide a false representation of love that is dictated by emotions or stipulations to be together forever.

Seed for Thought: When was the last time the Father was able to captivate your mind with hidden treasures written inside the Bible? Proverbs 24:14 (NIV) "In the same way, wisdom is sweet to your soul. If you find it, you will have a bright future, and your hopes will not be cut short." You will never know what exciting and thrilling story written inside the Bible will add adventure to your life and help you develop an intimate relationship to learn…

Who I truly AM!

"I am the Alpha and the Omega, the First and the Last, the Beginning and the End."
Revelation 22:13 (NIV)

The mystery of God has always been an area many people struggle to grasp to believe. How a loving, compassionate, and merciful God could bring judgment and condemnation to a world created during the breaking ground (Chapter One). The ability to understand God and how He operates. Man must seek Him daily in prayer, asking for wisdom to comprehend, why the God we serve can administer love and judgment at the same time. Hosea 4:6 (NIV) says, "My people are destroyed from lack of knowledge. Because you have rejected knowledge, I also reject you as my priests; because you have ignored the law of your God, I also will ignore your children." Lack of knowledge concerning who God is and all the benefits that come with serving Him, in my opinion, is the main reason why people struggle. God does not want to turn a deaf ear to our situation or withdraw love from

His creation. But because the world is choosing to turn a deaf ear or not love Him back to fulfill the sinful pleasure of the flesh is the reason judgment is being cast upon this world today. The world is ignoring all visible warning signs that one day the Father will descend from Heaven, riding a white horse called Faithful and Truth. He will then bring justice while judging us to determine if war needs to happen in this world (Revelation 9:11-12). Until He returns, the Holy Spirit (Comforter) will remain on the scene, drawing and leading all humbled hearts back into the arms of a loving, compassionate, and merciful Father. Who chooses for now to show empathy (ability to understand) over apathy (lack of concern) towards all sheep gone astray or refuses to return to Him.

Seed for Thought: If God was to assess your life, would He have empathy or apathy toward you? (Exodus 33:19)

_____

_____

_____

_____

The story of the Prodigal Son, according to Luke 15:11-32. The youngest son asked his father for his share of the inheritance to leave home. He lost all his money on wild living. When a famine swept over the land, everyone was affected, including the youngest son. With no money in his pockets, he had no choice but to take a job feeding pig. The Prodigal Son became so hungry, the pods that the pigs ate sounded good to eat because no one would help him. The youngest son began to realize his father's hired servants ate better than he did, so he decided to return home. On the way home, he rehearsed in his mind what he would say to his father once he saw him. As the youngest son approached the Palace immediately, the father saw him and expressed empathy with a joyful spirit, that his son had finally come home. The father did not care; he squandered all his money. He ordered the servants to dress the youngest son in the most beautiful linen and throw a big celebration in his honor while the oldest son labored in the fields.

When the oldest son heard the party, he immediately stopped and went home. As the oldest son approached the Palace, he noticed a celebration going on in honor of his youngest brother. The oldest son did not have empathy but jealousy, rage, and anger towards his youngest brother. For years, he slaved for their father and never disobeyed him or received anything for his services. The oldest son wanted an answer to the question. Why was the youngest son being honored for living life wildly and squandering all his money? The father said to the oldest son, you were always there for me, and everything I possess belongs to you. We have to celebrate because your brother is not dead but alive; he once was lost, but now he is found.

In my opinion, the father decided to forgive and have compassion instead of focusing on the reasons why the youngest son chose to live a sinful life. We all, at some point throughout our lives, have gone astray to fulfill the sinful pleasure of the flesh. Praise God! Our Heavenly Father is patiently waiting with open arms to forgive, love, and embrace us when we return home. 1 John 1:9 (NLT) states, "But if we confess our sins to him, he is faithful and just to forgive us our sins and to cleanse us from all wickedness."

Seed for Thought: A sincere confession of our sin cleanses the heart and purifies the soul. Titus 3:4-7 (NIV) says, "But when the kindness and love of God our Savior appeared, he saved us, not because of the righteous things we had done, but because of his mercy. He saved us through the washing of rebirth and renewal by the Holy Spirit, whom he poured out on us generously through Jesus Christ our Savior, so that, having been justified by his grace, we might become heirs having the hope of eternal life."

Our Heavenly Father, since the beginning, has visibly revealed Himself to us. According to Romans 1:20 (NIV), "For since the creation of the world God's invisible qualities, his eternal power and divine nature have been clearly seen, being understood from what has been made, so that people are without excuse, to believe God does exist." Without His existence…

- Who do we believe wakes us up every morning when the alarm clock does not go off?
- Who do we believe provides oxygen in the atmosphere, so our lungs can be filled with air to keep breathing?
- Who do we believe allows our heart to beat day and night?
- Who do we believe heals our body when the doctor says there nothing else to be done?
- Who do we believe protects our children when we can't be around them 24/7?
- Who do we believe provides healing for our broken hearts, emotional, verbal, and physical scars while showing comfort to a family when a loved one passes away?

The only answer to all the questions ever asked is God. Psalm 100:3 (NLT) says, "Acknowledge that the Lord is God! He made us, and we are his. We are his people, the sheep of his pasture." God will forever provide compassion to the sick, healing ointment to all open wounds, and comfort during a loss. He will forever remind His children to breathe to survive while mercy covers us so that Satan won't destroy us. Grace will stay on the scene to keep pushing us to finish the race God originally planned for us (Psalm 86:15). We must understand, His love will forever reach the Heavens, and His faithfulness will forever stretch high as the skies (Psalm 108:4), and everything taken will be restored to the original plan. Joel 2:25-27 (NIV) says, "I will repay you for the years the locusts have eaten - the great locust and the young locust, the other locusts and the locust swarm - my great army that I sent among you. You will have plenty to eat, until you are full, and you will praise the name of the LORD your God, who has worked wonders for you; never again will my people be shamed. Then you will know that I am in Israel, that I am the LORD your God, and that there is no other; never again will my people be shamed." God is always working on our behalf, be patient, and just enjoy life. While waiting for the harvest, just praise, worship, and thank Him in advance until it comes.

Seed for Thought: Always remember the best is yet to come if we don't give up and grow weary during the wait. Ephesians 2:8-10 (NKJV) says, "For by grace you have been saved through faith, and that not of yourselves; *it is* the gift of God, not of works, lest anyone should boast. For we are His workmanship, created in Christ Jesus for good works, which God prepared beforehand that we should walk in them." Every time Satan starts to tell us that our Heavenly Father does not love us, rebuke him in Jesus' Name. We are God's children, and every well-disciplined child should be able to….

Hear the True Shepherd's voice

Now that we are starting to comprehend how much the Father truly loves us, it makes it easy to yield to the Holy Spirit (Comforter) to help us develop a deeper intimate relationship with the Father, so His voice sounds crystal clear in our ears. Jesus told the Pharisees, according to John 10:2-5 (NIV), "The one who enters by the gate is the shepherd of the sheep. The gatekeeper opens the gate for him, and the sheep listens to His voice. He calls his own sheep by name and leads them out. When he has brought out all his own, he goes on ahead of them, and his sheep follow him because they know his voice. But they will never follow a stranger; in fact, they will run away from him because they do not recognize a stranger's voice." What separates the Father's voice over other voices is His distinct and unique ability to bring joy and peace to our spirit that places a smile on our face and laughter in our soul. Psalm 119:103-104 (NKJV) says, "How sweet are Your words to my taste, Sweeter than honey to my mouth! Through Your precepts I get understanding; Therefore, I hate every false way" that may lead to destruction.

There is a lot of teaching in the world today that tells us God does not exist, or it's okay to worship a different god instead of the one true living God for us to be saved. Jesus tells us, according to John 10:7-10 (NIV), "Very truly I tell you, I am the gate for the sheep. All who have come before me are thieves and robbers, but the sheep have not listened to them. I am the gate; whoever enters through me will be saved. They will come in and go out and find pasture. The thief comes only to steal and kill and destroy; I have come that they may have life and have it to the full."

Through God's eyes, it does not matter if we serve in the Church or do not attend Church at all. Not having an intimate relationship with the Father means He does not know us even though He created us. Unfortunately, most people believe they have an abundance of time to get everything right, but truthfully tomorrow is not promised to anyone. If the Holy Spirit (Comforter) is not capable of making us believe, then turn on the television and watch the news (1 Peter 1:24-25). Once we experience the Father's unconditional love over false love, no one can convince us to serve another god or be in a relationship with someone who tries to alter our personality to fit into their world.

Seed for Thought: People place boundaries on us; the creator takes the limits off us to achieve our purpose, with perks to call His name anytime. What limitations have people set on you that keep you in bondage? (Galatians 4:6-7)

_____

_____

_____

_____

What's His Name?

Knowing His name allows the Holy Spirit (Comforter) to download the Father's **DNA** (**D**angerous a**N**d **A**nointed) into our spirit so we can proclaim to the world with boldness and confidence that my house and I will serve the Lord and no one else (Joshua 24:15). When we need one on one intimacy, calling the name **Abba** (Daddy) draws Him close to us. Saying the name **EloHim** shows the world He is reliable, mighty, and will reign forever over other gods (Jeremiah 31:33). Mentioning the name **El Eloah** tells the whole world God still exists and rules over the universe regardless if His creation chooses to take His name out of buildings and schools (Nehemiah 9:17). **El Shaddai** is not afraid to show His mighty right hand of power to anyone who's out of control (Genesis 49:24-26). While **El Olam** is the everlasting God (Psalm 9:1-3) and **Ehyeh**, the God who is unchangeable, especially when men try to water down the laws and commandments already established to accept behaviors that do not conform to God's image (Exodus 3:14). For right now, **our Father** chooses to show unconditional love to anyone who calls Him by any name written in the Bible. Such as...

- **Jehovah Jireh** – The Lord will Provide (Genesis 22:14)

- **Jehovah Rapha** – The Lord who Heals (Exodus 15:26)

- **Jehovah Shalom** – The Lord who gives Peace (Judges 6:24)

- **Jehovah Nissi** – The Lord is your Banner (Protector) (Exodus 17:15)

I challenge every reader to study in-depth all of God's names and their actual meaning; to fully understand who God is and what He stands for. Deuteronomy 6:4-8 (NIV) says, "Hear, O Israel: The LORD our God, the LORD is one. Love the LORD your God with all your heart and with all your soul and with all your strength. These commandments that I give you today are to be on your hearts. Impress them on your children. Talk about them when you sit at home and when you walk along the road, when you lie down and when you get up. Tie them as symbols on your hands and bind them on your foreheads." We never know the day or hour pulling out a Bible in public, might be our last with the way the world is going.

Seed for Thought: Studying God's word enhances our spiritual knowledge and boosts our spiritual growth. Psalm 119:15-16 (NLT) says, "I will study your commandments and reflect on your ways. I will delight in your decrees and not forget your word," to remember the…

Laws and Commandments

"Be strong and very courageous. Be careful to obey all the instructions Moses gave you. Do not deviate from them, turning either to the right or to the left. Then you will be successful in everything you do. Study this Book of Instruction continually. Meditate on it day and night so you will be sure to obey everything written in it. Only then will you prosper and succeed in all you do." Joshua 1:7-8 (NLT)

The laws and commandments written in the old testament were established after God delivered the Children of Israel out of Egypt (Exodus 6:2-9). While Israelites were wandering in the wilderness, they began to murmur and complain about everything. Eventually, they became impatient and started committing sinful acts. Moses was commanded by God to establish the laws and commandments for the Children of Israel to follow if anyone sinned (Exodus 21-22; 23:1-19). The more the Children of Israel disobeyed and sinned, the more boundaries and guidelines God placed on them. Whenever God needed to give more instruction to Moses, God led him away from the camp to set up a Tent of Meeting. The Tent of Meeting was a holy place for Moses to worship and meditate on God. During those quiet times with the Lord, Moses received the Ten Commandments and the Major Offerings listed on the next several pages.

Seed for Thought: Having Godly Knowledge makes it easy not to be deceived by the world. Proverbs 14:6 (NIV) says, "The mocker seeks wisdom and finds none, but knowledge comes easily to the discerning."

The Ten Commandments

(Exodus 20:1-17 (ESV); Deuteronomy 5:4-21)

1. You shall have no other gods before me.
2. You shall not make for yourself an image in the form of anything in heaven above or on the earth beneath or in the waters below. You shall not bow down to them or worship them; for I, the Lord your God, am a jealous God, punishing the children for the sin of the parents to the third and fourth generation of those who hate me, but showing love to a thousand generations of those who love me and keep my commandments.
3. You shall not misuse the name of the Lord your God, for the Lord will not hold anyone guiltless who misuses his name.
4. Remember the Sabbath day by keeping it holy. Six days you shall labor and do all your work, but the seventh day is a sabbath to the Lord your God. On it you shall not do any work, neither you, nor your son or daughter, nor your male or female servant, nor your animals, nor any foreigner residing in your towns. For in six days the Lord made the heavens and the earth, the sea, and all that is in them, but he rested on the seventh day. Therefore, the Lord blessed the Sabbath day and made it holy.
5. Honor your father and your mother, so that you may live long in the land the Lord your God is giving you.
6. You shall not murder.
7. You shall not commit adultery.
8. You shall not steal.

9. You shall not give false testimony against your neighbor.

10. You shall not covet your neighbor's house. You shall not covet your neighbor's wife, or his male or female servant, his ox or donkey, or anything that belongs to your neighbor's.

Five Major Offerings

The Burnt Offering (Leviticus 1)

This type of offering requires a male animal or human whom God chose to sacrifice at the time. After the Israelites acknowledged their sin, a male animal with no defects was brought to the entrance of the tabernacle to kill. The sons of Aaron, who were the Chosen Priests, would have specific instructions for Moses by God, on what to do with the blood and the body after sacrifice (organs, skin, and bones). Once the whole process was complete. God was pleased, and a fresh start was given. God did not exempt man from this particular burnt offering. He just instructed and expected man to be obedient out of fear unto the Lord.

In Genesis 22:1-13, God ordered Abraham to place his son Isaac on the altar as a human burnt offering. Abraham was obedient and feared God, so he took Isaac to the place that was chosen by God. Abraham laid his son on the altar, took out a knife, and as he drew back his hand to kill Isaac, God immediately stopped Him. For his obedience, a ram was placed in the bush to sacrifice instead. God bestowed favor and honor to Abraham for being obedient, walking upright, and holy before the Lord (Psalm 84:11).

The Grain Offering (Leviticus 2)

This type of offering does not include a male animal or human sacrifice, but fine flour and oil. The individual sinning would take Aaron's son, the Priest, fine flour and oil to mix with incense to burn. If the aroma was pleasing to God, forgiveness would be granted. If a grain offering was baked in an oven and presented as a cake, no yeast added. The Priest would take out the memorial portion and place it on the altar. If God was pleased, the aroma would be pleasant to His nostrils. God also gave specific instructions concerning grain offering used as the first fruit and if it was acceptable to Him or not.

The Fellowship Offering (Leviticus 3)

This type of offering, a male or female animal without defect, is used to slaughter. The animal slaughtered is taken to the entrance of the Tent of Meeting. Then Aaron's sons, the Priests, give specific instructions on what to do with the blood and body parts (organs, skins, and bones). The kidneys and liver from the animal are placed on top of the burnt offering as an aroma pleasing to God. God also gave specific instructions in the chapter on what to do with other animals used as a religious sacrifice. God told the Israelites and every generation after them, how they were supposed to live and eat any food after disposing of any animal's fat and their blood.

The Sin Offering (Leviticus 4)

This type of offering, God gave Moses specific instruction concerning Israelite and Priest, who sinned unintentionally. Moses told the guilty individuals what to do and bring before the Lord to receive forgiveness. The person had to bring a young bull without defect and place it at the Tent of Meeting to slaughter. Then the anointed Priest would take the blood to the Tent of Meeting, dip his finger into the blood and sprinkle seven times before the LORD in front of the curtain of the sanctuary. The anointed Priest would follow the complete instruction as laid out, on what to do with the blood and the remaining inner parts (organ, skin, and bones) of the young bull sacrifice. In the same chapter, God gave complete instructions on what to sacrifice if the whole community and leaders were to sin. The anointed Priest, not God, would atone (restitute) the guilty person or parties for their sins before forgiving them.

The Trespass Offering (Leviticus 5)

This type of offering, God gives specific instructions on how to handle public charges that were brought against anyone who touches anything ceremonially unclean. It did not matter if the individual had an unclean spirit; once they became aware of their sin, they would be considered guilty. Once the individual confessed their guilt for committing a sinful act, they would have to bring before the LORD a female lamb or goat from the flock of the sin offering for the Priest to give an atonement (restitution) for their sins.

Now that we have learned some valuable information concerning the laws and commandments established in the Old Testament. I challenge all readers to go back and do an in-depth study of the Ten Commandments and the Offerings to understand the many different ways God established rules for the Children of Israel to redeem themselves after committing sinful acts. The laws and commandments in the Old Testament still apply to us today, except the Major Offerings were replaced with grace and mercy as we read about in the New Testament. If additional comprehension is needed to understand while reading the Old and New Testaments, ask the Holy Spirit (comforter) in prayer for understanding and wisdom to fully grasp the Father's words. Remember, people perish for lack of knowledge if they choose to remain quiet and not ask any questions for deeper comprehension.

Since the breaking ground (Chapter One), the Holy Spirit (Comforter) has been working 24/7 trying to draw lost souls back to the Father. Choosing not to learn about our wonderful Father and how much He truly loves us will eventually bring condemnation and judgment into our life and our children's children's life. The good news is right now; there is still time to get our life right. God desires no man or woman to perish but turn away from their sins and surrender completely. The Father is patiently waiting to reveal to the world Noble Men of Valor or Beautiful Butterflies transformed by the blood of Jesus Christ. Having Christ's **DNA** (**D**angerous a**N**d **A**nointed) spirit dwelling inside of us makes it easy for the world to see Christ, not us. (Ephesians 1:11-14). Being equipped with God's **DNA** (**D**angerous a**N**d **A**nointed) spirit embedded into our spirit means we now have nutrients of….

Wisdom for the Soul

1. "See what great love the Father has lavished on us, that we should be called children of God! And that is what we are" 1 John 3:1(NIV)!

2. "And so we know and rely on the love God has for us. God is love. Whoever lives in love lives in God and God in them" 1 John 4:16 (NIV).

3. "If anyone turns a deaf ear to my instruction, even their prayers are detestable" Proverbs 28:9 (NIV).

4. "This is how you can recognize the Spirit of God: Every spirit that acknowledges that Jesus Christ has come in the flesh is from God, but every spirit that does not acknowledge Jesus is not from God. This is the spirit of the antichrist, which you have heard is coming and even now is already in the world" 1 John 4:2-3 (NIV).

5. "A false witness will not go unpunished, and whoever pours out lies will not go free. Proverb 19:5 (NIV)."

6. "To all perfection I see a limit, but your commands are boundless. Oh, how I love your law! I meditate on it all day long. Your commands are always with me and make me wiser than my enemies" Psalm 119:96-98 (NIV).

7. "For the word of God is alive and active. Sharper than any double-edged sword, it penetrates even to dividing soul and spirit, joints and marrow; it judges the thoughts and attitudes of the heart. 13 Nothing in all creation is hidden from God's sight. Everything is uncovered and laid bare before the eyes of him to whom we must give account " Hebrews 4:12-13 (NIV).

8. "I have hidden your word in my heart that I might not sin against you" Psalm 119:11 (NIV).

9. "Therefore, since we have been justified through faith, we have peace with God through our Lord Jesus Christ, through whom we have gained access by faith into this grace in which we now stand. And we boast in the hope of the glory of God. Not only so, but we also glory in our sufferings, because we know that suffering produces perseverance; perseverance, character; and character, hope. And hope does not put us to shame, because God's love has been poured out into our hearts through the Holy Spirit, who has been given to us" Romans 5:1-5 (NIV).

10. "Call on you, my God for you will answer me; turn your ear to me and hear my prayer. Show me the wonders of your great love, you who save by your right hand those who take refuge in you from their foes. Keep me as the apple of your eye; hide me in the shadow of your wings from the wicked who are out to destroy me, from my mortal enemies who surround me" Psalm 17:6-8 (NIV).

Seed for Thought: Father, I ask you to open up our hearts to fully comprehend who you truly are. I ask you, Father, to expand our knowledge as you equip and turn us into Noble Men of Valor or Beautiful Butterflies able to fully blossom into our destiny. This prayer I ask in Jesus' Name, Amen.

Personal Reflection

_____
_____
_____
_____
_____
_____
_____

Chapter Seven

Full Bloom

"I have been crucified with Christ; it is no longer I who live, but Christ lives in me; and the life which I now live in the flesh I live by faith in the Son of God, who loved me and gave Himself for me." Galatians 2:20 (NKJV)

As God's plans begin to unfold before our eyes, focusing on the Father is essential to keep moving forward into kingdom assignment. Satan is aware of God's plans for our lives and will do whatever it takes to stop us from reaching our destiny. Apostle Paul encouraged the Philippians to stay the course when He told them, "Brethren, I do not count myself to have apprehended; but one thing I do, forgetting those things which are behind and reaching forward to those things which are ahead, I press toward the goal for the prize of the upward call of God in Christ Jesus"(Philippians 3:13-14 NKJV).

Pressing forward into kingdom assignment should be the goal of all Christians, but we allow Satan to distract us with Egypt, people, material possessions, and even self. Always remember, God will never lure anyone back to Egypt. He will only direct us to handle unfinished business before moving forward into kingdom assignment. If God does allow us to go back to Egypt, peace will guide us everywhere we go. His grace will cover us from the crown of our head to the soles of our feet. His mercy will forgive us every time we stumble and fall. His love will send like-minded Christians to encourage us along the journey when our spirits are low and His joy will keep a constant smile on our face. While the Holy Spirit (Comforter) will continue equipping us for battle and protecting us from all obstacles to make sure we stay grounded and rooted in the word of God (2 Thessalonians 3:3). It does not matter if God is leading us out of Egypt or moving us into new territory; nothing or no one can stop the kingdom assignment God designed for our life (John 15:7).

Seed for Thought: We never blossom when life is easy, but only when adversity is faced. The Holy Spirit (Comforter) comes along and gives us spiritual guidance to increase our faith to help us finish this race we call life. Having faith in the size of a mustard seed makes it easy to tell all mountains to move, which stands in our way (Luke 17:6).

Spiritual Guidance

"For this reason we also, since the day we heard it, do not cease to pray for you, and to ask that you may be filled with the knowledge of His will in all wisdom and spiritual understanding; that you may walk worthy of the Lord, fully pleasing Him, being fruitful in every good work and increasing in the knowledge of God; strengthened with all might, according to His glorious power, for all patience and longsuffering with joy; giving thanks to the Father who has qualified us to be partakers of the inheritance of the saints in the light."

Colossians 1:9-12 (NKJV)

Spiritual guidance is knowledge obtained from reading God's word that transforms the mind, body, and spirit into Noble Men of Valor or Beautiful Butterflies. The transformation changes the perspective on how to deal with different situations and people until we start to see ourselves as a prosperous individual in every area of our lives. Even close family and friends will begin to see the change in us. There was a man named Mike, who loved God but allowed people and fear to control his life. While attending a Christian class, Mike rededicated his life back to Christ. After surrendering, a supernatural anointing overpowered Mike causing his mind, body, and spirit to be transformed and renewed by the blood of Jesus.

When the class was over, Mike decided to visit his family in Jacksonville, Florida. At the beginning of the family gathering, everyone assumed Mike's conversation would only be about his past failures and mistakes. Instead, the family noticed a humble, grateful, and thankful young man of God, who loved life with a deep passion for God. Mike's best friend mentioned that he could see a spiritual glow illuminating through him. When the family event was over, Mike went back to his hotel room to prepare for his trip home. In the bedroom, Mike began to reflect on the positive comments spoken by his family and best friend. Immediately his heart was filled with joy and peace. No longer was he bound by his past failures or mistakes; instead, he was fully restored and known by God. Mike's transformation changed his perspective of himself and how he viewed others (Fictional Story).[8]

I challenge every reader to reflect on their first encounter with the Father. Then ask yourself this one question: Am I still on fire for the Lord, or have I let life burn out the fire that made me an effective witness? After truthfully answering the question, pray and ask the Holy Spirit (Comforter) to relight the fire inside of you or keep the light that's already ignited burning forever. Also, if any reader has never experienced an intimate encounter with the Father after reading this book, it will happen (1Peter 2:1-3).

Seed for Thought: Being an effective witness for the Lord not only helps us but touches other people's lives. Deuteronomy 10:12-13 (NIV) is a great scripture reference to use as a spiritual guidance tool to become an effective witness. Let's briefly discuss:

- **To fear the LORD, your God** means to always be mindful of His presence at all times, so we are held accountable for our conversation, thought, and action. The Holy Spirit's (Comforter) job is to make sure we fear God, remain humble and live a righteous life according to the standard written in the Bible. Psalm 86:11(NLT) says, "Teach me your ways, O Lord, that I may live according to your truth! Grant me purity of heart, so that I may honor you" (Proverbs 22:4).

- **To walk in obedience to Him** means being able to listen and submit to a higher authority over self by allowing the Holy Spirit (Comforter) to teach us how to love other people regardless if they treat us wrong. Being obedient to God releases healing into our hearts, joy into our spirit, and peace into our soul. Exodus 19:5 (NLT) says, "If you will obey me and keep my covenant, you will be my own special treasure from among all the peoples on earth; for all the earth belongs to me" (John 14:15; Psalm 128:1).

- **To love Him** means placing God first above everything and everybody in our life. His love changes our whole identity, builds our self-confidence, and opens up our minds to receive possibilities and new opportunities that present themselves. He teaches us how to express love and how to tell the difference when a person is expressing genuine love and when they are not. Exodus 34:14 (NIV) says, "Do not worship any other gods, for the LORD, whose name is Jealous, is a jealous God" (Psalm 73:25-26; Matthew 5:8).

- **To serve the LORD your God with all your heart and with all your soul** means to have a heartbeat rhythm in sync with God to the point that serving others becomes automatic without expecting nothing in return but to see them happy and feeling loved. Matthew 6:20-21 (NIV) says, "But store up for yourselves treasures in heaven, where moths and vermin do not destroy, and where thieves do not break in and steal. For where your treasure is, there your heart will be also."

- **To observe the LORD's commands and decrees that I am giving you today for your own good?** Allows us to serve with a humble heart, trust in His Word, and believe He will always have our back 24/7. He promises if we follow His commandments, everything will be restored to the original plan before we were born. Psalm 37:23-24 (NIV) says, "The LORD makes firm the steps of the one who delights in him; though he may stumble, he will not fall, for the LORD upholds him with his hand."

The bible is full of scriptures we can use as spiritual guidance tools. Here are just a few additional scriptures to use: Matthew 25:40, Hebrews 13:2, Proverbs 16:16, and Mark 11:25. Spiritual guidance teaches us how to demonstrate love to everyone we meet daily. Whether it is giving a hug, a smile, a compliment, saying hello or even asking someone how their day is going. These are just some simple ways to demonstrate God's love. Another way spiritual guidance is demonstrated is through hospitality. Here are a few suggestions:

- Show Love to new members who join the Church or rededicate their life back to Christ by helping the Church cook meals for them.

- If someone is struggling financially, offer to buy their groceries, or treat the individual and their family to a meal.
- When someone doesn't have a car, offer to give the individual or their entire family a ride to an appointment, Church, or the grocery store.
- Any single parents offer to babysit their kids to give them a break.

Whenever you demonstrate love towards others, always use wisdom. First, seek the Father in prayer daily so the Holy Spirit (Comforter) can direct our path to do everything with a pure heart. Staying connected to the Father makes it easy to follow His commandment and "love your neighbor as yourself" (Galatians 5:14). Jesus knew if he did not petition to the Father on our behalf for help and protection, we would struggle today to love others and follow every commandment established by God (John 17:6-19). What exciting news to all Chosen vessels!! No longer do we live in fear, wondering what could happen to us if we step out on faith to live according to the Father's plans. Chosen vessels, with the help of the Holy Spirit (Comforter), we are anointed mighty warriors, sealed and equipped with the blood of Jesus to rise above adversity and soar into our destiny.

Chapter Eight

New Beginning

The Start of something new releases hope into the spirit that something great is about to happen in the future.

A new beginning in the Lord eliminates our past and creates a fresh start for us. According to Isaiah 43:18-19 (NIV), "Forget the former things; do not dwell on the past.

See, I am doing a new thing! Now it springs up; do you not perceive it? I am making a way in the wilderness and streams in the wasteland." When we allow the Holy Spirit (Comforter) complete access to our life, we permit the Father to teach us how to reflect, not dwell, while moving forward into the promise already laid out for us through our ancestors Abraham, Isaac (son), and Jacob (grandson). The commitments include turning our ashes back into crowns of beauty, sadness into joy, and despair to constant praise that overflows from our hearts (Isaiah 61).

Stop right now and allow the Holy Spirit (Comforter) to point out any past mistakes or failures not released to the Father or already delivered from and then picked back up. After the Holy Spirit (Comforter) makes us aware of our mistakes or failures, release everything to the Father to rid them out of your life forever. While waiting ... be still, praise, trust, and lean closer to the Father until deliverance is complete. Psalm 46:10 (NIV) says, "Be still and, and know that I am God." Keep in mind, sometimes new beginnings with God can start rocky and slow due to other weeds (sins) that may hinder us from genuinely walking into our destiny. When the Holy Spirit (Comforter) believes we are ready to receive our harvest, the Father will receive a green light to release everything stored up in Heaven and specifically designed for us today (Numbers 23:19).

Seed for Thought: Readers, as you read God's promises given to our ancestors on the next page, praise and thank Him for what He has in store for you once your newness begins. Proverbs 15:30 (NLT) says, "A cheerful look brings joy to the heart; good news makes for good health."

God's Promises (Ancestors)

Abraham Promises- Genesis 22:15-18 (NLT)

"This is what the Lord says: Because you have obeyed me and have not withheld even your son, your only son, I swear by my own name that I will certainly bless you. I will multiply your descendants beyond number, like the stars in the sky and the sand on the seashore. Your descendants will conquer the cities of their enemies. And through your descendants all the nations of the earth will be blessed all because you have obeyed me."

Isaac's (son) Promise- Genesis 26:12-15 (NLT)

"When Isaac planted his crops that year, he harvested a hundred times more grain than he planted, for the Lord blessed him. He became a very rich man, and his wealth continued to grow. He acquired so many flocks of sheep and goats, herds of cattle, and servants that the Philistines became jealous of him. So the Philistines filled up all of Isaac's wells with dirt. These were the wells that had been dug by the servants of his father, Abraham."

Jacob's (grandson) Promise-Genesis 28:13-15 (NLT)

"I am the Lord, the God of your grandfather Abraham, and the God of your father, Isaac. The ground you are lying on belongs to you. I am giving it to you and your descendants. Your descendants will be as numerous as the dust of the earth! They will spread out in all directions to the west and the east, to the north and the south. And all the families of the earth will be blessed through you and your descendants. What's more, I am with you, and I will protect you wherever you go. One day I will bring you back to this land. I will not leave you until I have finished giving you everything I have promised you."

God's Promises (Us)

If the promises mentioned on the previous page, do not easily convince you, take a few minutes to read Deuteronomy 7:11-15 (NIV) to fully understand God's promises for us. "Therefore, take care to follow the commands, decrees and laws I give you today. If you pay attention to these laws and are careful to follow them, then the LORD your God will keep his covenant of love with you, as he swore to your ancestors. He will love you and bless you and increase your numbers. He will bless the fruit of your womb, the crops of your land—your grain, new wine and olive oil—the calves of your herds and the lambs of your flocks in the land he swore to your ancestors to give you. You will be blessed more than any other people; none of your men or women will be childless, nor will any of your livestock be without young. The LORD will keep you free from every disease. He will not inflict on you the horrible diseases you knew in Egypt, but he will inflict them on all who hate you."

Seed for Thought: Stop right now and reflect on God's promises for you today. How does that make you feel? Does it give you hope for a bright future and eagerness to start your kingdom assignment? Do you feel you are not worthy to receive God's best for your life? Why? (Proverbs 16:3)

Until our harvest is released, God will test and stretch our faith to see if we have released everything over to Him. God wants to make sure we are standing on His word, trusting and believing Him during every trial. Isaiah 42:8-9 (NLT), "I am the Lord; that is my name! I will not give my glory to anyone else, nor share my praise with carved idols. Everything I prophesied has come true, and now I will prophesy again. I will tell you the future before it happens." To prove God does test and stretch our faith. In Daniel, Chapter 3 Shadrach, Meshach, and Abednego had to demonstrate to God and non-believers, they were completely sold out to God's truth and righteous laws and commandments written in the Bible. The men refused to bow down and worship an image made of gold created by King Nebuchadnezzar. When the King saw the three men were strong in their beliefs, he ordered Shadrach, Meshach, and Abednego to be placed in a fiery furnace that was seven times hotter than normal. The three men stayed focused on God by trusting and believing every word promised to them. After being bound, restrained, and placed in the fiery furnace. To King Nebuchadnezzar's amazement, when he looked into the furnace, he noticed not three, but four men standing in the heated furnace. Shadrach, Meshach, and Abednego's new beginning happened after the King proclaimed the fourth man looks like the son of God. King Nebuchadnezzar also gave praises to Shadrach, Meshach, and Abednego's God, then issued a decree of consequences to any nation or language spoken against their God. The three men received their harvest of prosperity after doors of opportunities opened to promote the men to a higher rank.

Seed for Thought: When God's **DNA** (**D**angerous a**N**d **A**nointed) spirit is intermingled in our bloodline, favor is released into our life. God does not always come when we call Him, but He is still on time (Deuteronomy 10:14-22).

Every test passed shows God we are ready to be elevated to the next level in His Powerful Anointed Army.[9] During every inspection, any sinful behavior found is removed and embedded with healthy nutritional supplements to revitalize our weak foundation. All dreams or vision seeds crushed by Satan are replanted back into a healthy mind. New soil of mulch is added daily to the foundation to preserve new healthy roots from Satan's devices used to damage the roots. God's love and guidance will sprinkle water and rays of sunshine onto the seeds, commanding them to grow and produce stems with buds of baby roses (prosperity). Periodically, God will inspect the spirit to see if there are other infected areas needed trimming away. If found, God will prune back any corrupted roots before adding additional healthy mulch to cover-up the hollow spaces until new roots grow in its place. Keep in mind the pruning process could take years or even decades to remove or trim weeds (sins).

When God is ready, a seal of approval stamp is placed on us before presenting to the world a beautiful, elegant, fully bloomed Rose, transformed by God. The world will no longer see **(say your birth name)** but a new creation fully transformed by the Blood of Jesus. Once we reach this point in the transformation process, our new beginning will cause doors of new opportunities to open, which produce financial stability and spiritual growth. Those new opportunities will create a domino effect to affect other people's lives to draw back lost souls to Christ forever.

Final Words

Readers, God's ultimate plan, was orchestrated in the book of Genesis when life was blown into the dirt to form man before Satan weeds (sins) altered God's plans. Before Revelation takes place, the Holy Spirit (Comforter) is roaming the land, calling everyone home to grant permission to the Father so he can place the individual on the Potter's wheel for transformation into a Chosen vessel used in God's Army. God needs our help!! In the Bible, God used twelve men with different personalities and skill sets to transform into disciples as Chosen vessels. God also chose throughout the Bible an alcoholic, stutterer, prostitute, adulterer, murder, tax collector, and a persecutor of Christians, besides other willing men, women, and children less qualified, according to the Pharisee and Sadducees standards, as Chosen vessels. In the present, God is still using the same qualifications and skill sets of people to transform into nonconformist radicals as modern-day Chosen vessels.

God is calling again; all modern-day Chosen vessels to assist with the training of our future generation of Chosen vessels. If we attend Church but don't actively serve God, it's time to commit. If we are not a member of a spirit-filled Bible-believing Church, get serious and join a God-fearing Church today. All qualified Chosen vessels are locking arms with God to create one mighty big army to destroy Satan in the last days. I ask all readers to allow our creator to remove any corrupted layers during the transformation process, so God can use us in the Kingdom before we receive the promises that were promised to us by God through our ancestors.

Seed for Thought: Do you believe you are a Chosen vessel? If your answer is yes, God's love is waiting with open arms to place you on the Potter's wheel called A Rose: The Layers In A Transformation Process.

Appendix

1. The bold letters, in the color red, represent the Father's blood that flows through our veins in the form of **DNA** (**D**angerous a**N**d **A**nointed). God's **DNA** is shown throughout the entire book through the color red. When you visibly see the rose petals on the cover of the book or see the many names or words associated with the Father, Son, and Holy Spirit.

2. Jesus was the first Chosen vessel used by the Father to spread light into a dark world. The Father throughout the Bible Chose many vessels, and even today, He still is choosing Chosen vessels to finish the work Jesus started. Capitalizing the letter "C" in Chosen means the Father has placed a seal of approval on all vessels transformed by the blood of Jesus to be used by God to do a mighty work for the Kingdom.

3. The Breaking Ground is significant to when God created the beginning in Genesis Chapter One.

4. All Baggage Reclaim quotes are an unknown author.

5. Capitalizing the words Love, Joy, Peace, Patience, Kindness, Goodness, Gentleness, Self-Control, and Faithfulness represents the Fruit of Spirit, which is shown through forty miracles performed by Jesus during the three years of His ministry of preaching and teaching the Gospel.

6. Capitalizing Noble Man of Valor or Beautiful Butterflies identifies the Chosen vessel's status after Christ has transformed the individual. The Chosen vessels are refined and reshaped on the Potter's Wheel into God's image. An image that has the same authority as Jesus to call on the Father in prayer by us His words in the Bible to fight all battles faced.

7. Answers Key:

    A) Obedience B) Forgive C) Gentleness D) Righteous E) Truth F) Self-Control G) Humble H) Patience I) Compassion J) Love

8. This story represents a new beginning to an individual after he has surrendered and allowed Christ to transform his mind, body, and spirit into the image of Christ.

9. His Powerful Anointed Army made up of Spirit-filled believers who are not afraid to stand boldly on the battlefield, winning souls and fighting the good fight until Christ returns without being ashamed of the Gospel.

Personal Reflection

Personal Reflection

Personal Reflection

Made in the USA
San Bernardino, CA
05 July 2020